# *Amici Curiae* and Strategic Behavior in State Supreme Courts

# *Amici Curiae* and Strategic Behavior in State Supreme Courts

SCOTT A. COMPARATO



PRAEGER

Westport, Connecticut
London

**Library of Congress Cataloging-in-Publication Data**

Comparato, Scott A. (Scott Alson)
*Amici Curiae* and strategic behavior in state supreme courts /
Scott A. Comparato.
p. cm.
Includes bibliographical references and index.
ISBN 0-275-97827-3 (alk. paper)
1. Courts of last resort—United States—States. 2. *Amici Curiae*—United States. 3. Judicial process—United States. I. Title.
KF8736.C64 2003
347.73'26—dc21 2003046385

British Library Cataloguing in Publication Data is available.



Library of Congress Catalog Card Number: 2003046385
ISBN: 0-275-97827-3

First published in 2003

Praeger Publishers, 88 Post Road West, Westport, CT 06881
An imprint of Greenwood Publishing Group, Inc.
www.praeger.com

Printed in the United States of America

The paper used in this book complies with the Permanent Paper Standard issued by the National Information Standards Organization (Z39.48–1984).

10 9 8 7 6 5 4 3 2 1

For Angela
This is as much yours as it is mine

# Contents

# Illustrations

TABLES

FIGURES

# Acknowledgments

I would like to take the time to thank the many people who helped me throughout the process of writing this book. I have benefited from the advice and assistance of faculty, fellow graduate students, friends and family. I am thankful for the support and advice of professors and fellow students at Washington University where I began this work in the form of my dissertation. My work is improved because of their efforts, and I am richer as a scholar and a person for having studied with them. I would like to thank my advisor, Lee Epstein, for her patience and guidance throughout my graduate career. She served as a demanding and honest mentor, providing me with an excellent example of what it means to be a successful teacher and scholar. I am also thankful for the support and advice of Valerie Hoekstra, Jack Knight, Bill Lowry, and Bob Salisbury. They read previous versions of this project always providing timely and helpful suggestions.

I also want to thank a number of colleagues with whom I studied at Washington University. Brady Baybeck, Andy Duttlinger, Tim Johnson, Barbara Kinsey, Andrew Martin, Scott McClurg, Chris Ostella, Anne Peterson, and Beth Wilner all offered their friendship and professional advice at various stages of this project. It is a rare case of writer's block that cannot be remedied by beer, good conversation, and a game of darts.

I also want to thank my family for their support. Explaining to them what it is I do and why I do it has always served to keep me grounded and focused. Most importantly, I am thankful for the love and friendship of my wife, Angela Reinoehl. She has been an enthusiastic supporter of my work, and her love and kindness have helped keep me going when I doubted myself. Without her steadying influence, it would not have been possible for me to succeed in this effort.

# CHAPTER 1

# *Amici Curiae* and State Supreme Court Justices

## INTRODUCTION

> *Amicus Curiae* is a Latin phrase for "friend of the court" as distinguished from an advocate before the court...It serves only for the benefit of the court, assisting the court in cases of general public interest..., by making suggestions to the court..., by providing supplementary assistance to existing counsel..., and by insuring the complete and plenary presentation of difficult issues so that the court may reach a proper decision...
>
> —Judge Robert Hemphill, Senior Judge of the U.S. District Court for the District of South Carolina, in Alexander v. Hall[1]

In September of 1997, Supreme Court Justice John Paul Stevens spoke before the Chicago Bar Association on their 125th Anniversary. During his address, Stevens recalled his tenure as a member of the Bar Association Committee that screened the qualifications of candidates for judicial office. Commenting on the importance of that committee and its role, Stevens argued against strict popular election of judges at all levels:

> ...any selection and retention process that makes popularity the standard for measuring fitness for judicial office creates an unacceptable risk of conflict between the judge's duty to apply the law impartially and his or her interest in retaining office.[2]

He concluded his remarks by arguing that popular election may be the best method for selecting other political actors, but that:

> ...when we need neutral arbitrators to resolve bitterly contested disputes between private citizens, or controversies between an individual and the State,

> those arbitrators should be chosen by a process that preserves their freedom to act independently. The thousands and thousands of Cub fans who have repeatedly visited Wrigley Field this season undoubtedly know much more about the rules of baseball and the ability of the National League umpires to apply them fairly, than most voters know about the law or the qualifications of judges... Nevertheless, I think that you would agree that the home team fans should not have the authority to hire and fire umpires.[3]

Stevens was arguing for judicial selection mechanisms that would limit the role of the public in selecting judges. He felt that the judicial selection system used was important in that, depending on how justices were chosen, they would be accountable to constituencies that would limit their ability to act impartially and independently.

Stevens's references to constituencies is reminiscent of James Madison's warnings of the mischiefs of faction in the *Federalist #10.* Making judges accountable to the people would invite abuse by powerful individuals or groups interested in pursuing their interests through the legal system. As Stevens's comments make clear, the courts are not immune from influence by powerful segments of the population, and making members of the courts electorally accountable only serves to make them more susceptible to such influence.

Stevens's concern is that elected judges are more easily influenced by the arguments made by groups, given their perceived lower levels of job security. Whether or not his fears are well founded, groups do participate before the courts through the filing of *amicus* briefs, lobbying for a particular outcome. The nature of that lobbying, and its effect on judicial behavior, drives this research. What are groups saying and how are judges responding?

Scholars have posited that interest groups play a similar and universal role; regardless of whether they are lobbying Congress or the courts, they are the transmitters of information to policymakers.[4] Supplying information to political decision-makers allows groups to attain their policy and group maintenance goals. One forum in which groups can achieve these goals is through participation as *amicus curiae* in state supreme courts. *Amici* are able to provide information, through the arguments in their briefs, to state supreme court justices about particular issues of law, the preferences of other political actors, and possible policy implications of the courts' decisions.

I make use of *amicus curiae* briefs submitted in state supreme courts to evaluate the effects of state level institutions on the types of information provided to state supreme court justices. Specifically, I focus on the following questions arising from two possible constraints on judicial and group behavior: (1) How do state judicial selection mechanisms affect the types of information provided by groups in *amicus* briefs? (2) How does the ballot initiative, a mechanism that allows the public to override decisions of state supreme courts, influence the content of information provided by groups in their *amicus* briefs? and (3) What, if any, effect do these institutional mechanisms have on the behavior of state supreme court justices?

In the remainder of this chapter, I present the basic framework of strategic accounts to explain the behavior of state supreme court justices and interest groups that are discussed in greater detail in Chapter 2. I assume that both groups and state supreme court justices are strategic actors, with groups motivated by the attainment of policy and group maintenance, and state supreme court justices by policy and the continued maintenance of their position on the court. I argue that the information provided in *amicus curiae* briefs allows both groups and state supreme court justices to achieve their respective goals. These models permit me to derive expectations about the behavior of these actors. In the final section of the chapter, I describe the ways in which I operationalize these hypotheses and outline the balance of the book.

## A STRATEGIC THEORY OF JUDICIAL BEHAVIOR

Judges play a vital role in the policy-making process. In order to gain a better understanding of how they interact with other political actors, I offer a theory of judicial decision making that suggests that justices behave strategically. Strategic approaches to judicial decision making have been used by a number of scholars of the Supreme Court in recent years.[5] Others, focusing on state supreme courts, adopt strategic approaches to explain the decision making of state supreme court justices.[6] Whether the focus is on the U.S. Supreme Court or state supreme courts, these researchers assume that justices recognize that the attainment of their goals, regardless of what those goals are, is dependent on the preferences of other actors and what actions they expect those actors to take.

### Justices and Their Goals

Studies of judicial behavior have generally focused on the Supreme Court. Not surprisingly, most discussions of judicial goals have taken the Supreme Court as their primary focus as well.[7] Some of these studies suggest that judges may have one or more goals, including career enhancement,[8] making good policy,[9] and avoiding Supreme Court reversal.[10] I adopt the position forwarded by Epstein and Knight,[11] that a primary goal of all justices is to see the law reflect their policy preferences. Others accept policy as a primary goal for state supreme court justices as well.[12]

Further, the literature suggests that state supreme court justices are influenced by their electoral situation and see electoral security as an important goal.[13] Unlike federal judges, state supreme court justices must run for reelection on a regular basis. Though there is evidence to suggest that incumbent state supreme court justices enjoy a high level of electoral security, those that serve in competitive election states may feel more vulnerable than justices in retention election states, where justices run against their own record.[14]

In this regard, state supreme court justices are similar to members of Congress. It has been shown that electoral arrangements influence the behavior of members of Congress.[15] Some argue that reelection is the primary goal of members of Congress,[16] while others recognize that the creation of good public policy is a motivation for members as well.[17] As a result, members of Congress pursue strategies that will maximize their chances for reelection.

Though state supreme court justices enjoy high reelection rates, scholars have argued that these public officials are also concerned about voter reprisal.[18] In a number of states, judicial elections are competitive, with narrow margins of victory for incumbents.[19] Despite this apparent perception of their electoral security, recent work by Hall shows that retention elections in particular are actually becoming less competitive.[20]

## Strategic Behavior by State Supreme Court Justices

Justices may have multiple goals, but for state supreme court justices, I argue that reelection and policy goals are of foremost importance. However, they are not free to vote their sincere preferences. The strategic model holds that they do not make decisions based solely on their ideological preferences. They understand that in order to achieve their goals, they must account for the potential actions of other actors. At the state level, supreme court justices may consider the views of their colleagues on the bench, the state legislature, the governor, the bureaucracy, and the public.[21] State supreme court justices may also consider the possible reactions of actors on the federal level, most prominently the Supreme Court. All of these actors, to varying degrees, have the ability to influence the efficacy of the decisions made by state supreme courts.

Justices wish to see their personal policy preferences enacted, but the strategic account suggests that they do not make decisions based solely on their ideological attitudes; justices realize that the ability to achieve their goals is dependent upon the actions of other actors. Justices act strategically in pursuit of policy when they account for the preferences and possible actions of those actors.

## Constraints on Judicial Behavior

When applying the strategic approach to decision making, it is crucial to understand the institutional arrangements that affect the decisions of justices. Two institutions in particular are expected to influence state judicial behavior: state judicial selection systems and the ballot initiative. State supreme court justices, unlike federal judges, do not enjoy life tenure. There are five primary methods used to select and retain state supreme court justices. These methods are designed to make justices accountable, with varying degrees of effectiveness, to different constituencies. I expect that these differences in judicial selection will influence the behavior of both justices and groups.

In addition to the judicial selection method used, the ballot initiative, a mechanism that allows the public a direct role in the policy making process, should also contribute to the decision-making calculus of state supreme court justices. State supreme court justices are not free to vote their sincere preferences; they must account for the institutional environment when making decisions. Interest groups must also be aware of the institutional environment and prepare their *amicus* briefs to capitalize on these institutions to achieve their goals.

## A STRATEGIC THEORY OF INTEREST GROUP BEHAVIOR

The preceding discussion suggests that State supreme court justices are strategic actors whose primary goals are the attainment of policy and reelection. The information that groups provide to State supreme court justices, in the form of *amicus curiae* briefs, assists them in obtaining these goals. In what follows, I discuss the goals of interest groups and how they act to achieve those goals through the filing of *amicus* briefs. In particular, the information contained in *amicus curiae* briefs aid groups in achieving the goals of group maintenance and policy attainment.

### Goal Orientation

Robert Salisbury defines an interest group as "...an organized association which engages in activity relative to governmental decisions."[22] Mark Petracca offers another, somewhat more specific, explanation of groups as "...membership- or nonmembership-based organizations or institutions that engage in activities to seek specific policy or political goals from the state."[23] Both of these definitions, implicitly or explicitly, identify the primary goal of interest groups as the attainment of favorable governmental policy for their members.

Scholars that have discussed group goals have done so within the context of lobbying activities directed at Congress. Implicit in most discussions of lobbying is the idea that groups are interested in securing favorable policy.[24] The particular policy position a group takes can be the result of the leadership acting at the behest of its membership or as a reflection of the preferences of group leadership.[25] However the policy position of a group is determined, a primary objective of virtually all groups is to participate successfully in the policy-making process.

Some scholars have suggested that considerations other than the attainment of policy can serve as significant motivation for groups.[26] One of these is certainly the continued existence and prosperity of the group itself.[27] It is in the interest of the decision makers and leaders of the group to continue to provide benefits to its members in order to maintain sufficient levels of support, financial and otherwise, to participate in the activities chosen by leaders to best obtain their preferred policies.

### Strategic Behavior by Interest Groups

Interest groups are motivated by policy and group maintenance and they act strategically to attain those goals. They make calculations about the environment in which they are operating and follow strategies that maximize their chances for success. One of the primary methods used by groups to achieve their policy and maintenance goals is by providing information to relevant policy makers.

State supreme courts have become increasingly attractive forums for groups to pursue their policy and maintenance goals. They may participate as direct sponsors of litigation or through the filing of *amicus curiae* briefs. Filing *amicus* briefs has the advantage that it is a relatively inexpensive way to participate in the legal system, especially when compared with litigating directly. Groups need not devote nearly the amount of time and money that the litigants in a case are forced to expend. This allows groups to target those cases that will help them achieve their goals most effectively, using their resources most effectively. Participating as *amicus curiae* also allows groups to participate in multiple forums simultaneously, letting them publicize their causes more efficiently.

Filing *amicus* briefs in multiple forums, possibly simultaneously, assists groups in keeping current members and attracting new members. It is critical for groups to maintain, or grow, membership levels so that they are able to continue pursuing strategies to achieve their policy goals. An effective way for groups to do that is participating in the courts in a highly visible way through the filing of *amicus* briefs.

## INTEREST GROUPS AND THE IMPORTANCE OF INFORMATION

Information transmission to critical policy makers is crucial for interest groups. However, groups are limited in the ways that they are able to provide information when participating in the courts. They are limited to the briefs filed, as litigants or *amici*, and through oral argument. Given their limited ability to provide information to the courts, groups must maximize their opportunities when provided with the opportunity to participate before the courts.

Interest group scholars have paid substantial attention to the role played by interest groups as information providers.[28] Much of the recent work on the transfer of information by groups has focused on their efforts aimed at legislators.[29] A major concern with policy makers relying on the information provided by groups is the possibility that groups would use their expertise in specific issue areas to misrepresent and manipulate the information that they provide. Most policy makers do not have the time or resources to independently obtain this information or, in some cases, to check the accuracy of the information provided to them by groups. The incentive for groups to manipulate information to their own advantage is tempered by the concern that other groups will provide conflicting information. Groups rely on their reputations as reliable providers of information in order to gain access, and possibly influence, with legislators and judges. As a result, given the large number of groups providing information to policy makers, on a wide variety of issues, it is unlikely that groups will provide false or misleading information. Groups are motivated by their policy and maintenance goals, and engaging in misrepresentation has the potential to seriously hamper their ability to achieve those goals.

In order to pursue these goals effectively, groups must gain influence with the courts. Strategic policy-seeking groups are motivated to position themselves in such a way as to send particular messages to policy makers.[30] One way that groups may improve the likelihood that the arguments they provide will be used by state supreme court justices is through repeated participation as *amicus* in order to develop reputations as reliable providers of relevant information. Over time, *amicus* briefs filed by groups may come to be relied on by justices for the arguments they contain. Some scholars question how much justices refer to *amicus* briefs when making their decisions,[31] but it is this commitment by groups to the development of long term strategies that may distinguish the degree to which justices rely upon the information provided by groups.

Clearly, information transmission is crucial for interest groups, but when participating in litigation, they are limited in the ways that they can provide information to justices. *Amici* have more freedom to present information that assists them in pursuing their policy and maintenance goals. However, if groups expect to effectively achieve these goals, they must provide information that allows justices to achieve their goals as well.

### Interest Groups and Institutions

When discussing the strategic behavior of interest groups, the argument is similar to that of the strategic behavior of justices, though differences should be noted. Again, it is critical to understand the institutional context when evaluating the behavior of groups. Distinct from judicial behavior, there are numerous ways that groups can act strategically in the legal system. Groups make choices regarding in which venues to participate, whether to directly sponsor litigation or to file *amicus* briefs, and which cases to participate in as *amicus*. However, the focus here is on the strategic choices made by groups after they have already decided to participate in state supreme courts as *amicus*. The question regarding strategic behavior is what types of information groups choose to provide in their *amicus* briefs.

Groups are not necessarily able to see their policy positions put into law in all circumstances. They must also concern themselves with institutional constraints and will tailor the arguments in their *amicus* briefs to maximize their chances to obtain favorable policy. They may take into account the judicial selection mechanisms used in states and whether the public has the opportunity to directly overturn decisions of the state supreme court through the ballot initiative.

The institutional setting may also influence the information provided by *amici* for other reasons. As I stated earlier, groups are also motivated by maintenance concerns. There may be instances where groups would not expect that their participation as *amicus* will result in a policy outcome favorable to the group and its membership. In such instances, group goals may still be served through participation as *amicus*. By showing members (and potential members) that they are active in particular forums and in particular policy domains, they may be able to retain current members and attract new members. Success may be less important than an open and active presence on particular issues and in certain arenas. In such instances the types of information provided by *amici* may differ from that from groups participating because they expect favorable policy as a likely or possible result of their participation. Thus, the institutional setting may have implications for those groups participating as *amicus*.

## *AMICUS* BRIEFS AND JUDICIAL BEHAVIOR

Institutional arrangements are important for understanding the behavior of groups and state supreme court justices. Institutions structure the choices made by state supreme court justices and interest groups by altering the incentives of those actors. The judicial selection system will affect the reelection and policy goals of state supreme court justices, as well as the policy and maintenance goals of interest groups. I anticipate that the ballot initiative and referendum will influence the reelection and policy goals of state supreme court justices as well as the policy and maintenance goals of interest groups. This discussion suggests that the ability of state supreme court justices and groups to attain their goals is affected by the institutional setting in which they operate. This leads to a number of expectations.

## Information Provision by Interest Groups

The focus in this study is on the strategic nature of information transmission by groups. I assume that groups do indeed behave strategically to attain their goals of group maintenance and favorable policy. Groups will be most likely to provide information that they feel will be most important to the justices on the court. This will differ depending on the institutional structure of the state. In Figure 1.1, I lay out the expectations for both *amicus* and group behavior based on the judicial selection mechanisms of the states. Additionally, Figure 1.2 shows the expectations of group and judicial behavior based on the presence of the ballot initiative in states. The models motivate the following discussion of the behavior by both *amici* and state supreme court justices.

Given these selection systems, I argue that state supreme court justices will be most accountable to those to whom they are ultimately responsible for their jobs. In partisan election states that is the electorate and in legislative appointment states, that is the state legislature. This can be viewed as a continuum from most to least accountable to the electorate. As a result, state supreme court justices will be most interested in obtaining information about the policy implications of their decisions on the public in those states where there is the most proximate electoral connection with the public. This connection lessens as we move to the right on the continuum toward systems where the electoral connection to the public is less proximate.

In addition, I expect that the judicial selection mechanisms will affect the types of arguments that groups will provide in their *amicus* briefs. Specifically, cases will contain the most arguments about policy in partisan election states and the least amount in legislative appointment states. Research shows that judicial elections in partisan election states are generally the most competitive,[32] and as a result, information about the preferences of the public and their potential reactions to the decisions of the court will be of most use to state supreme court justices in those states.

I have the opposite expectation for group behavior regarding institutional arguments. While state supreme court justices should want information about the policy implications on the public to the left of the continuum, as we move to the right, they should become more concerned about the preferences and possible actions of other state actors. As a result, groups should provide the most arguments about institutional actors in legislative appointment states and the least in partisan election states. I place the legislature to the right of the governor on the continuum for two reasons. First, in many states, the powers of the governor are quite limited, and the ability of the governor to initiate any effort to overturn a decision of the state supreme court is constrained, and even if able to mobilize such an effort, he or she would still need the assistance of the legislature. Second, legislatures in most states, in addition to their ability to pass statutes

Figure 1.1
Expected Accountability of State Supreme Court Justices Based on Judicial Selection Method

| | Judicial Selection Method | | | | |
|---|---|---|---|---|---|
| | Partisan Election | Non-Partisan Election | Merit Selection | Gubernatorial Appointment | Legislative Appointment |
| **Judicial Accountability** | ← Most Accountable to Electorate | | | | Most Accountable to Institutions → |

Figure 1.2
Expected Behavior of Groups Based on Judicial Selection Method

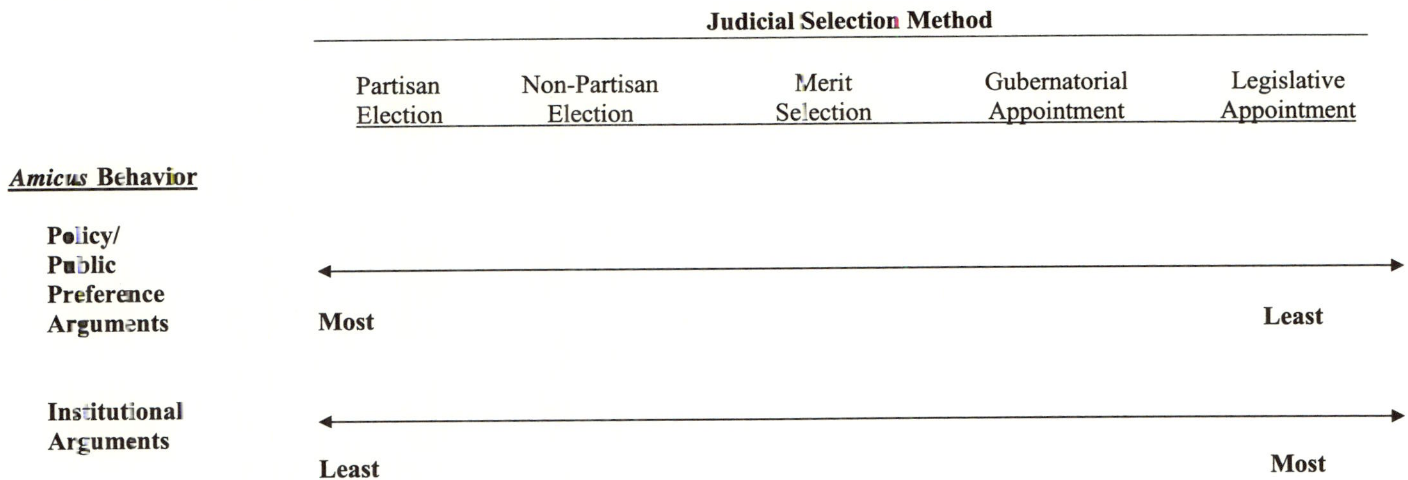

or begin efforts to amend the constitution, have the ability to pass referenda, a mechanism effectively equivalent to the ballot initiative, though it is started by member(s) of the legislature rather than the public.

While I expect the reelection system used by a state to influence judicial and group behavior, I also anticipate that the ballot initiative will influence the behavior of state supreme court justices and groups. The initiative is a formal mechanism that allows the public a direct role in policy making and the ability to override the decisions of state supreme courts. State supreme court justices will be more accountable to the electorate in those states with the initiative than in those states that lack the initiative. As a result, groups will make more arguments about policy in those states with the initiative and more arguments about institutional actors in states without the initiative.

In states that allow the use of the ballot initiative, and with retention elections, *amici* will be more likely to present information that alerts justices to the preferences of the legislature and the likelihood that efforts will be made to initiate a referendum. Where the state legislature is the body with the authority to override decisions of the state supreme court, I expect that justices and interest groups will be cognizant of that fact, and groups will provide information that will alert the justices of the preferences and possible actions of the legislature. This information will be useful to the justices, allowing them to make considerations about how best to achieve their most preferred policy while at the same time avoiding conflict with the legislature that might lead to unwanted negative publicity that might endanger their retention chances in the next election.

Across all states, *amici* will be more likely to provide arguments based on state statutes and state constitutions in order to allow justices to base their decisions on state law. In the late 1970s, some of the more liberal members of the Supreme Court, fearing that the increasingly conservative Court would undo many of the decisions of the liberal Warren Court, called on state jurists to rely on their own constitutions and precedent in reaching liberal decisions, in order to avoid review by the Supreme Court, thus hopefully preserving those changes made in the law by the Court in the previous twenty years. Justice O'Connor responded to this attempt by the liberal wing of the Court several years later, warning state supreme court justices that, unless their decisions relied on their state constitutions exclusively, the Supreme Court would assume that the U.S. Constitution applied, allowing for Supreme Court review. As a result of O'Connor's admonishment, I expect that *amici* will be more likely to rely on state constitutions, statutes, and precedent than on the U.S. Constitution and federal statutes.

### The Influence on Judicial Votes

Given the theoretical expectations outlined for groups and the information contained in their briefs, I next turn to the resulting behavior of state supreme court justices. Justices will want information that assists them in achieving their policy and reelection goals. Where *amici* alert justices to the particular policy preferences of segments of the electorate and of other political institutions, state supreme court justices are more likely to vote in accord with what that information is telling them. Across all states, justices will be more likely to respond to the information from the briefs of interest groups than that provided by other actors. Clearly, groups that participate before the court on a regular basis are more likely to have developed a reputation for expertise and reliability, thereby increasing their chances of having the court rely upon the information they provide.

One of the primary goals of this work is to investigate the relationship between institutions and judicial decision making. In addition to analyzing the briefs for their content, it is a central goal of this research to determine whether the *amicus* briefs that are filed result in a greater likelihood of success for those parties that they support. Do certain parties, making specific arguments, enjoy greater success in some settings than in others? As I have already discussed, justices on the state level face institutional constraints that may influence their decision making. In other words, due to their electoral exposure, judges on the state level may be swayed by interests arrayed on one side of a particular issue, while their federal counterparts would not be so influenced. Therefore, interest groups should be more successful than others, and in particular, when *amici* support the position of one of the litigants in a case, that party should have an advantage over those without such support.

## RESEARCH DESIGN

To assess these predictions, I examine a sample of cases in which there is at least one *amicus* brief filed on the merits in state supreme courts between 1986 and 1995, resulting in approximately 650 total cases. I identify seven states with different institutional dimensions and obtain data from each state with the particular institutional structures. Table 1.1 lists the states, the judicial selection method used in that state, and whether the state allows for the ballot initiative.

State supreme court justices in South Carolina are chosen and subsequently retained by a direct of vote of the members of the state legislature. South Carolina does not provide for direct input by the electorate through the ballot initiative. In Alabama, justices are elected directly by the electorate through the partisan ballot, and like South Carolina, Alabama does not allow the public the direct opportunity to alter decisions of the state supreme court through the ballot initiative.

A number of states elect state supreme court justices via non-partisan ballots, and unlike the states discussed above, there are several that allow for public participation through the ballot initiative. Specifically, Wisconsin elects judges by the non-partisan ballot and provides for the ballot ini-

**Table 1.1**
**Judicial Selection, Retention, and Constitutional Amendment Mechanisms**

| State | Initiative | Selection Mechanism | Retention Election |
|---|---|---|---|
| Alabama | No | Partisan | No |
| Colorado | Yes | Merit | Yes* |
| Kansas | No | Merit | Yes |
| Michigan | Yes | Non-Partisan | No |
| Wisconsin | No | Non-Partisan | No |
| New Jersey | No | Gubernatorial Appointment | No |
| South Carolina | No | Legislative Appointment | No |

*Justices in merit system states, once appointed, serve a short first term prior to their first retention election. Once retained, they face retention elections on a regular basis.

tiative. Michigan, while electing justices by the non-partisan ballot, does not use the ballot initiative.

Numerous other states have done away with the direct election of judges by the public. Twenty-one states choose supreme court justices through the Missouri, or merit plan. Under the merit plan, independent judicial commissions provide the governor with a list of names of potential candidates from which to choose to fill the vacancy. Once initially selected by the governor, justices regularly face the voters in retention elections. There is also variation in merit plan states in their willingness to allow the public direct involvement through the ballot initiative. Colorado provides for the ballot initiative. The state of Kansas, while selecting justices by the merit plan, does not use the ballot initiative.

Finally, several states allow the governor to choose state supreme court justices without the intervention of judicial nominating commissions. These states, largely from the Northeast, do not provide for the ballot initiative, with the exception of Massachusetts. New Jersey was chosen because data were more readily available and it does not allow for the ballot initiative. Therefore this is the only state from which data will be drawn with this institutional character. This leaves a total of seven states to be included in the analysis.

In order to evaluate the previous predictions about *amicus* activity, it is necessary to obtain several types of data from the states: arguments in *amicus* briefs, arguments in litigant briefs, and the outcomes of the cases with *amicus* participation. First, I collect and code the arguments in *amicus curiae* briefs. It would be cost prohibitive, and ultimately unnecessary, to copy the entire *amicus* brief to glean the arguments made. I copy the

"Cover Page," "Table of Contents" (which includes the arguments), "Table of Authorities," and "Conclusion" of each brief. I also copy the "Statement of Interest" or "Introduction" when they are present in the brief. By copying these sections of the brief, I am able to gain purchase on the arguments made by the *amicus,* what legal authority they rely on in making their arguments, and what party (if any), the *amicus* supports.

In order to draw conclusions about the effects of institutions on group behavior, I code the *amicus* briefs for several types of information. These categories will be discussed at length in later chapters, but the most important categories of information are: (1) the policy consequences of a decision; and (2) the preferences of the other branches of state government. These are the primary types of information that are hypothesized to be of use to state supreme court justices, and it is expected that the information provided in *amicus* briefs will vary depending on the institutions present. As I mentioned, this is not a complete list of the variables that are coded, but it does offer a sample of some of the kinds of information that may be of importance to state supreme court justices, and will likely be provided by *amici* in their briefs.

In sum, the information that is necessary to assess the behavior of state supreme court justices and groups is available but must be obtained from the states themselves, either from state archives or law libraries. The remainder of the data can be obtained from other sources, including regional case reporters, newspapers, and the LEXIS electronic database. This information will be sufficient to assess my predictions of strategic behavior by both state supreme court justices and interest groups.

## SIGNIFICANCE OF RESEARCH

From this research, I expect to gain a better understanding of the effects that institutions have on the behavior of interest groups as third parties on the state level. Central to strategic accounts of judicial decision making is the role of information, and how justices obtain information about the preferences and probable actions of other actors. *Amicus curiae* briefs serve an important function for justices, both on the federal and state level, providing them with useful information that allows them to pursue their policy preferences. Clearly there are important institutional differences between the federal and state courts, as well as differences between states. I argue that these institutions lead to differences in behavior, both by groups and justices, across states. It is these institutions that produce a situation in which *amicus* briefs are important for groups involved in the legal process at the state level, as well as the justices who read them.

This research contributes to a greater understanding of several fields of study. First, it adds to the interest group literature, providing a greater understanding of the behavior of groups at the state level. There has been a dearth of research on group advocacy in state supreme courts and this work advances our understanding of how groups participate as third parties in those courts. Second, it contributes to the work conducted on judicial decision making. Much has been written in this area. However, the bulk of that work has been conducted with federal courts as their focus. This work will add to that through the examination of decision making on the state level. There are substantial institutional differences between states that allow me to gain leverage on judicial behavior that would not be possible through an analysis of federal courts. Third, it contributes to the federalism literature, by examining the differences in institutional structures of states and the results that this has on the behavior of political actors in those states. The particular advantage of this work in this respect is the ability to evaluate the impact of institutional differences on the behavior of *amici* and the arguments that they make to state supreme court justices.

## ORGANIZATION OF THE BOOK

In Chapter 2, I discuss the importance of information and *amicus* briefs to both justices and groups. I expand on the theoretical foundation, discussing strategic accounts that focus on the behavior of U.S. Supreme Court justices and extrapolating from these to provide a strategic theory to explain the behavior of state supreme court justices. I provide a strategic account of group behavior that rests on the assumption that groups are motivated by policy concerns and the need to retain members. I then offer a brief discussion of the interest group environment in the states.

I move from a discussion of theoretical foundations that motivate this work, to a discussion in Chapter 3 of the original data used to test my theories of judicial and group behavior. I outline the types of cases included in the analysis, the method of collection, and the coding scheme used to evaluate the information contained in the briefs.

The goal of Chapter 4 is to determine whether the institutional mechanisms hypothesized to be of importance correlate with the information provided in litigant and *amicus* briefs. There are theoretical reasons for believing that litigants will provide different types of information in their briefs than that provided by *amici*. Litigant goals will differ substantially from the goals of *amici*, and the specific information that they provide in their briefs should differ as well, though state level legal and political institutions are also important for understanding what kinds of information they will provide. In addition to showing how the arguments vary according to the differences in institutions, these data are used to provide evidence that *amici*, across states, are more likely to make certain kinds of arguments than others.

In Chapter 5, I shift from an analysis of the information provided by *amici* and direct parties to an examination of the behavior of state supreme court justices. However, in this chapter, the emphasis is on whether the provision of certain types of information by litigants and *amici* impact the decision making of state supreme court justices. The goal of this chapter is to evaluate not only whether the arguments themselves influence the decisions of the justices, but also whether it matters who makes the arguments and whether they are made by multiple *amici* and litigants. Several sources of data are used for this chapter. In addition to the data collected from litigant and *amicus* briefs, I use data on the frequency of *amicus* participation, as well as data on the outcome of cases where *amicus* briefs are filed.

My purpose here is to evaluate whether interest groups and state supreme court justices behave strategically, through an analysis of *amicus* briefs and the decisions of state supreme court justices. In the concluding chapter, I summarize the results of the analysis from the previous chapters on both groups and state supreme court justices and explore the implications that institutional structure has on the behavior of political elites. I also discuss the importance of legal argumentation and why it is important that scholars of the courts turn their attention to this component of the legal process in order to better understand judicial outcomes.

## NOTES

1. *Alexander v. Hall* (64 F.R.D. 152, 1974).

2. John Paul Stevens. Speech delivered at the 125th Anniversary of the Chicago Bar Association, September 16, 1998.

3. Stevens, Speech to the Chicago Bar Association.

4. Raymond Bauer, Ithiel de Sola Pool, and Anthony Lewis Dexter. 1963. *American Business and Public Policy.* New York: Atherton; David B. Truman. 1951. *The Governmental Process: Political Interests and Public Opinion.* New York: Knopf; David Austen-Smith and John R. Wright. 1992. "Competitive Lobbying for a Legislator's Vote." *Social Choice and Welfare* 9:229–257; David Austen-Smith and John R. Wright. 1994. "Counteractive Lobbying." *American Journal of Political Science.* 38: 25–44; David Austen-Smith. 1993. "Information and Influence: Lobbying for Agendas and Votes." *American Journal of Political Science* 37: 799–833; Lee Epstein and Jack Knight. 1998. *The Choices Justices Make.* Washington, DC: CQ Press; John R. Wright. 1996. *Interest Groups and Congress: Lobbying, Contributions, and Influence.* Boston: Allyn and Bacon.

5. Lee Epstein and Jack Knight. 1998. *The Choices Justices Make.* Washington, DC: CQ Press; William N. Eskridge Jr. 1991. "Overriding Supreme Court Statutory Interpretation Decisions." *Yale Law Journal* 101: 331–417; William N. Eskridge Jr. 1991. "Reneging on History? Playing the Court/Congress/President Civil Rights Game." *California Law Review* 79: 613–84; John Ferejohn and Barry Weingast. 1992. "The Limitation of Statutes: Strategic Statutory Interpretation." *Georgetown Law Journal* 80: 565–582; Rafael Gely and Pablo Spiller. 1990. "A Rational Choice Theory of Supreme Court Statutory Decisions with Applications to the *State Farm* & *Grove City* Cases." *Journal of Law, Economics and Organization* 6: 263–300.

6. Paul Brace and Melinda Gann-Hall. 1990. "Neo-Institutionalism and Dissent in State Supreme Courts." *Journal of Politics* 52: 54–70; Melinda Gann-Hall. 1987. "Constituent Influence in State Supreme Courts: Conceptual Notes and a Case Study." *The Journal of Politics* 49: 1117–24; Melinda Gann-Hall. 1992. "Electoral Politics and Strategic Voting in State Supreme Courts." *Journal of Politics* 54: 427–46; Melinda Gann-Hall and Paul Brace. 1989. "Order in the Courts: A Neo-Institutional Approach to Judicial Consensus." *Western Political Quarterly* 42: 391–407; Melinda Gann-Hall and Paul Brace. 1992. "Toward an Integrated Model of Judicial Voting Behavior. *American Politics Quarterly* 20: 147–68; Melinda Gann-Hall and Paul Brace. 1994. "The Vicissitudes of Death by Decree: Forces Influencing Capital Punishment Decision Making in State Supreme Courts." *Social Science Quarterly* 75: 136–51; Pablo T. Spiller and Richard G. VandenBergh. 1997. "A Positive Theory of State Supreme Court Decision Making." Paper presented at the 1997 annual meeting of the Midwest Political Science Association, Chicago, IL.

7. Lawrence Baum. 1994. "What Judges Want: Judges' Goals and Judicial Behavior." *Political Research Quarterly* 47: 749–768; Lee Epstein and Jack Knight. 1999. "Mapping Out the Strategic Terrain: The Informational Role of *Amici Curiae*." In *Supreme Court Decision-Making: New Institutional Approaches,* eds. Howard Gillman and Cornell W. Clayton. Chicago: University of Chicago Press.

8. Mark A. Cohen. 1992. "The Motives of Judges: Empirical Evidence from Antitrust Sentencing." *International Review of Law and Economics* 12: 13–30; Harold W. Elder. 1987. "Property Rights Structures and Criminal Courts: An Analysis of State Criminal Courts." *International Review of Law and Economics* 7 (June): 21–32.

9. Sheldon Goldman. 1975. "Voting Behavior on U.S. Courts of Appeals Revisited." *American Political Science Review* 69: 491–506.

10. Jeffrey A. Segal, Donald R. Songer, and Charles M. Cameron. 1994. "The Hierarchy of Justice: Testing a Principal-Agent Model of Supreme Court-Circuit Court Interactions." *American Journal of Political Science* 38: 673–696.

11. Lee Epstein and Jack Knight. 1999. "Mapping Out the Strategic Terrain: The Informational Role of *Amici Curiae*." In *Supreme Court Decision-Making: New Institutional Approaches,* eds. Howard Gillman and Cornell W. Clayton. Chicago: University of Chicago Press.

12. Melinda Gann-Hall. 1987. "Constituent Influence in State Supreme Courts: Conceptual Notes and a Case Study." *The Journal of Politics* 49: 1117–24; Melinda Gann-Hall. 1992. "Electoral Politics and Strategic Voting in State Supreme Courts." *Journal of Politics* 54: 427–46.

13. Paul Brace and Melinda Gann-Hall. 1990. "Neo-Institutionalism and Dissent in State Supreme Courts." *Journal of Politics* 52: 54–70; Melinda Gann-Hall. 1987. "Constituent Influence in State Supreme Courts: Conceptual Notes and a Case Study." *The Journal of Politics* 49: 1117–24; Melinda Gann-Hall. 1992. "Electoral Politics and Strategic Voting in State Supreme Courts." *Journal of Politics* 54: 427–46; Melinda Gann-Hall and Paul Brace. 1989. "Order in the Courts: A Neo-Institutional Approach to Judicial Consensus." *Western Political Quarterly* 42: 391–407; Melinda Gann-Hall and Paul Brace. 1992. "Toward an Integrated Model of Judicial Voting Behavior." *American Politics Quarterly* 20: 147–68; Melinda Gann-Hall. 2001a. "State Supreme Courts in American Democracy: Probing the Myths of Judicial Reform." *American Political Science Review* 95(2): 315–330.

14. Melinda Gann-Hall. 1987. "Constituent Influence in State Supreme Courts: Conceptual Notes and a Case Study." *The Journal of Politics* 49: 1117–24; Melinda Gann-Hall. 1992. "Electoral Politics and Strategic Voting in State Supreme Courts." *Journal of Politics* 54: 427–46; John T. Wold and John H. Culver. 1987. "The Defeat of the California Justices: The Campaign, the Electorate, and the Issue of Judicial Accountability." *Judicature* 70: 348–55; Richard A. Watson, and Ronald G. Downing. 1969. *The Politics of Bench and Bar: Judicial Selection under the Missouri Nonpartisan Court Plan.* New York: Wiley; William Hall and Larry Aspin. 1987. "What Twenty Years of Judicial Retention Elections Have Taught Us." *Judicature* 70: 340–47.

15. David R. Mayhew. 1974. *Congress: The Electoral Connection.* New Haven, Conn.: Yale University Press; Morris P. Fiorina. 1974. *Representatives, Roll Calls, and Constituencies.* Lexington, Mass.: Lexington Books; Richard Fenno. 1973. *Congressmen in Committees.* Boston: Little, Brown; Douglas R. Arnold. 1990. *The Logic of Congressional Action.* New Haven: Yale University Press; John W. Kingdon. 1981. *Congressmen's Voting Decisions.* 2d. ed. New York: Harper & Row.

16. David R. Mayhew. 1974. *Congress: The Electoral Connection.* New Haven, Conn.: Yale University Press.

17. Richard Fenno. 1973. *Congressmen in Committees.* Boston: Little, Brown.

18. Thomas E. Mann. 1978. *Unsafe at Any Margin: Interpreting Congressional Elections.* Washington, DC: American Enterprise Institute for Public Policy Research; Gary C. Jacobson. 1987. "The Marginals Never Vanished: Incumbency and Competition in Elections to the U.S. House of Representatives, 1952–1982." *American Journal of Political Science* 31: 126–41; Melinda Gann-Hall. 1987. "Constituent Influence in State Supreme Courts: Conceptual Notes and a Case Study." *The Journal of Politics* 49: 1117–24; Melinda Gann-Hall and Paul Brace. 1989. "Order in the Courts: A Neo-Institutional Approach to Judicial Consensus." *Western Political Quarterly* 42: 391–407.

19. Philip L. Dubois. 1980. *From Bench to Ballot: Judicial Elections and the Quest for Accountability.* Austin: University of Texas Press; but see also Melinda Gann-Hall. 2001a. "State Supreme Courts in American Democracy: Probing the Myths of Judicial Reform." *American Political Science Review* 95(2): 315–30; Melinda Gann-Hall. 2001b. "Voluntary Retirements from State Supreme Courts: Assessing Democratic Pressures to Relinquish the Bench." *Journal of Politics* 63 (4): 1112–40.

20. Hall, "State Supreme Courts in American Democracy;" Hall, "Voluntary Retirements from State Supreme Courts."

21. Melinda Gann-Hall. 1987. "Constituent Influence in State Supreme Courts: Conceptual Notes and a Case Study." *The Journal of Politics* 49: 1117–24; Melinda Gann-Hall. 1992. "Electoral Politics and Strategic Voting in State Supreme Courts." *Journal of Politics* 54: 427–46; Melinda Gann-Hall and Paul Brace. 1994. "The Vicissitudes of Death by Decree: Forces Influencing Capital Punishment Decision Making in State Supreme Courts." *Social Science Quarterly* 75: 136–151.

22. Robert Salisbury. 1975. "Interest Groups." In *Handbook of Political Science, Vol. 4,* eds. Fred I. Greenstein and Nelson W. Polsby. Reading, Mass.: Addison-Wesley, p. 175.

23. Mark Petracca. 1992. "The Rediscovery of Interest Group Politics." In *The Politics of Interests: Interest Groups Transformed,* ed. Mark P. Petracca. Boulder, CO: Westview Press, p. 7.

24. Jeffrey Birnbaum. 1992. *The Lobbyists.* New York: Times Books; John Mark Hansen. 1991. *Gaining Access: Congress and the Farm Lobby, 1919–1981.* Chicago: University of Chicago Press; Laura Langbein. 1986. "Money and Access: Some Empirical Evidence." *Journal of Politics* 48: 1052–62; Kay Lehmann Schlozman and John Tierney. 1986. *Organized Interests and American Democracy.* New York: Harper & Row; John R. Wright. 1996. *Interest Groups and Congress: Lobbying, Contributions, and Influence.* Boston: Allyn and Bacon.

25. Mancur Olson. 1965. *The Logic of Collective Action.* Cambridge: Harvard University Press.

26. Jeffrey M. Berry. 1977. *Lobbying for the People.* Princeton, NJ: Princeton University Press; Terry Moe. 1980. *The Organization of Interests.* Chicago: University of Chicago Press; Mancur Olson. 1965. *The Logic of Collective Action.* Cambridge: Harvard University Press; Kay Lehmann Schlozman and John Tierney. 1986. *Organized Interests and American Democracy.* New York: Harper & Row; Robert H. Salisbury. 1969. "An Exchange Theory of Interest Groups." *Midwest Journal of Political Science* 3:1–32; Robert H. Salisbury. 1990. "The Paradox of Interest Groups in Washington, DC: More Groups and Less Clout." In *The New American Political System,* 2d version, ed. Anthony S. King. Washington, DC: American Enterprise Institute; James Q. Wilson. 1973. *Political Organizations.* New York: Basic Books.

27. Mancur Olson. 1965. *The Logic of Collective Action.* Cambridge: Harvard University Press; Terry Moe. 1980. *The Organization of Interests.* Chicago: University of Chicago Press; Robert H. Salisbury. 1969. "An Exchange Theory of Interest Groups." *Midwest Journal of Political Science* 3:1–32; Jack L. Walker. 1983. "The Origins and Maintenance of Interest Groups in America." *American Political Science Review* 77: 390–406.

28. David B. Truman. 1951. *The Governmental Process: Political Interests and Public Opinion.* New York: Knopf; Raymond Bauer, Ithiel de Sola Pool, and Anthony Lewis Dexter. 1963. *American Business and Public Policy.* New York: Atherton; Kay Lehmann Schlozman and John Tierney. 1986. *Organized Interests and American Democracy.* New York: Harper & Row; John Mark Hansen. 1991. *Gaining Access: Congress and the Farm Lobby, 1919–1981.* Chicago: University of Chicago Press; Jeffrey M. Berry. 1997. *The Interest Group Society,* 3rd. ed. New York: Longman.

29. David Austen-Smith and John R. Wright. 1992. "Competitive Lobbying for a Legislator's Vote." *Social Choice and Welfare* 9:229–57; David Austen-Smith and John R. Wright. 1994. "Counteractive Lobbying." *American Journal of Political Science* 38: 25–44; David Austen-Smith. 1993. "Information and Influence: Lobbying for Agendas and Votes." *American Journal of Political Science* 37: 799–833; John R. Wright. 1996. *Interest Groups and Congress: Lobbying, Contributions, and Influence.* Boston: Allyn and Bacon.

30. Wright, *Interest Groups and Congress,* p. 78.

31. See James F. Spriggs and Paul J. Wahlbeck. 1997. "*Amicus Curiae* and the Role of Information at the Supreme Court." *Political Research Quarterly* 50: 365–86; Epstein and Knight, "Mapping Out the Strategic Terrain"; Gregory A. Caldeira and John R. Wright. 1988. "Organized Interests and Agenda Setting in the U.S. Supreme Court." *American Political Science Review* 82: 1109–27; Gregory A. Caldeira and John R. Wright. 1990a. "The Discuss List: Organized Interests and Agenda-Setting." *Law and Society Review* 24: 807–36; Gregory A. Caldeira and John R. Wright.

1990b. "*Amici Curiae* Before the Supreme Court: Who Participates, When, and How Much?" *Journal of Politics* 52: 782–806.

32. Lawrence Baum. 1983. "The Electoral Fates of Incumbent Judges in the Ohio Court of Common Pleas." *Judicature* 66:42–50; Hall, "State Supreme Courts in American Democracy: Probing the Myths of Judicial Reform."

# CHAPTER 2

# Theories of Judicial and Interest Group Behavior

## INTRODUCTION

In this chapter, I further define and explain the theoretical foundations that underlie this research. Specifically, I develop a strategic model of decision making for state supreme court justices. I argue that they are rational actors, whose primary goals are reelection and the attainment of policy. The strategic model stands in contrast to the attitudinal model, which suggests that jurists are motivated to vote in accordance with their strict policy preferences.[1] I provide a detailed discussion of these two models of behavior, which have been applied most notably to Supreme Court justices, and extrapolate that work to construct a strategic model of state judicial behavior. I also offer a similar theoretical explanation for the behavior of interest groups.

## THEORIES OF SUPREME COURT BEHAVIOR

Before laying out the tenets of a strategic theory of state supreme court behavior, it is important to understand the research tradition from which this theory emanates. For some time the dominant model of decision making for U.S. Supreme Court justices has been the attitudinal model. However, in recent years, strategic approaches to the study of Supreme Court behavior have been advanced, resulting in a rethinking of how justices on the nation's highest court make decisions. In order to better understand the foundations that underlie the strategic theory of state supreme court behavior that I advance, a discussion of the attitudinal and strategic models that have been offered to explain U.S. Supreme Court behavior is essential.

### The Attitudinal Model

I argue that state supreme court justices are constrained by other branches of government and by specific institutional characteristics of state government. The electorate is able to override state supreme court decisions through the ballot initiative and the referendum. Additionally, state supreme court justices are constrained by those to whom they are ultimately responsible for their jobs. Unlike Supreme Court justices, most state supreme court justices are not appointed to their positions for life and must face either the electorate, or the members of the other branches of state government when running for reelection or retention.

The attitudinal model, a dominant paradigm for understanding the behavior of Supreme Court justices, was most coherently articulated and empirically tested by Jeffrey Segal and Harold Spaeth in *The Supreme Court and the Attitudinal Model*.[2] The basic tenets of the attitudinal model are that Supreme Court justices are goal-oriented political actors, who make decisions based on their own policy preferences expressed within the bounds placed on those preferences by the facts of the case being decided. Justices are able to express their individual policy preferences because of two important institutional features attached to the office the justices hold: life tenure and the separation of powers. Because justices are appointed for life and are not accountable to any particular constituency, they are free to vote their own policy preferences.[3] As the nation's highest court, the decisions of the Supreme Court cannot be appealed—their decisions are the final word on the issue. Because of these two institutional features, attitudinalists argue that members of the Supreme Court are free to vote their sincere preferences.

Segal and Spaeth recognize that the attitudinal model is theoretically grounded in the work of the legal realists of the 1920s and 1930s. Arising out of the elite law schools, realists such as Jerome Frank and Karl Llewellyn questioned the prevalent view of judicial decision making, advanced by the classical legal scholars of the time, suggesting that justices decide cases based solely upon the facts vis-à-vis precedent, the intent of the framers, the plain meaning of the Constitution and statutes, and the balancing of societal against constitutional interests.[4] To those scholars, law was:

> A complete and autonomous system of logically consistent principles, concepts and rules. The judge's techniques were socially neutral, his private views irrelevant; judging was more like finding than making, a matter of necessity rather than choice.[5]

While this staid and static view of the judicial function had prevailed among legal scholars for decades, the legal realists realized that judging was inherently a political function, and that judges did not merely "find" or "discover" the law through some jurisprudential treasure hunt. Indeed, judges *make* law. As Oliver Wendell Holmes said forty years before the work of Frank, Llewellyn, and other realists rose to prominence:

> The life of the law has not been logic: it has been experience. The felt necessities of the time, the prevalent moral and political theories [and] intuitions of public policy have had a good deal more to do than the syllogism in determining the rules by which men should be governed.[6]

Picking up on Holmes's view, the realists argued that though justices might use a number of approaches to arrive at their decisions, they serve merely as vehicles for the justices to advance their own preferences.[7] Missing from legal realism was an explicit discussion of judicial goals. The realists acknowledged that justices could adhere to numerous goals but did not incorporate any specific goal as predominant among justices.

It was not until C. Hermann Pritchett's *The Roosevelt Court*, published in 1948, that anyone argued that justices pursued policy as their primary goal in reaching decisions.[8] The impetus for Pritchett's work was his observation that dissent rates on the U.S. Supreme Court had steadily risen in the first half of the 20th century, a rise that was particularly striking in the 1930s and 1940s. Why, Pritchett asked, if they were simply applying rote rules of jurisprudence to case facts, would different justices come to different conclusions? If the legal model of decision making was indeed a valid explanation of judicial behavior, would not two different justices applying the same principles to the same facts reach similar conclusions? Pritchett reasoned that there was more at work than the realists presumed. While Frank, and other legal realists, suggested that judges actually invested something of themselves in the decision-making process, Pritchett concluded that it was the policy goals of the justices that led to the high dissent rates on the Court.

The idea that justices sought policy outcomes gained little immediate attention from social scientists, but in *The Judicial Mind* some seventeen years after Pritchett's seminal work, Glendon Schubert offered the first explicit model of judicial behavior predicated on the idea that attitudes drove observed behavior.[9] Relying upon theoretical advances by his contemporaries in the field of psychology, Schubert advanced a stimuli-response model that he used to scale justices along a continuum from liberal to conservative for specific policy issues.

While Rohde and Spaeth[10] offer the theoretical foundation for the attitudinal model, it did not gain its full power until the publication of Segal and Spaeth's book.[11] They expand on the work of Rohde and Spaeth, assuming that justices are interested in pursuing their own policy preferences. However, they contend that Supreme Court justices are able to pursue their policy preferences because they are appointed for life and therefore are not electorally accountable.[12] Because they control their own docket and presumably do not have ambition for higher office, justices are able to further their policy goals.[13] They concede that where lower court judges *are* electorally accountable, do not have complete control over their docket, and perhaps seek higher office, they may not be able to translate policy preferences into their decisions. The authors acknowledge that the attitudinal model rests squarely on the freedom of the justices to operate without fear of retribution from external sources such as the other branches of government or the public.

Segal and Spaeth deal with each of the tenets that support the model in turn. Since the Judiciary Act of 1925, the Supreme Court has enjoyed nearly total control over its docket. There are a small number of cases each term that the Court must hear as part of its responsibility as a court of original jurisdiction. They note that this requirement, though not sufficient, is a necessary condition for justices to vote their preferences.

Similarly, they note that at certain points in its history the Court did not enjoy a high level of prestige, and members were known to leave the bench for other political office.[14] Segal and Spaeth note that such ambitions are unlikely to be found among the Court's members these days.[15] Sitting on the Supreme Court is certainly considered to be the pinnacle of one's career for most involved in the legal profession and would therefore not be considered merely a stepping stone to a higher or more influential political office.

Lower court judges are also accountable to higher courts. Justices may not be willing to express their sincere policy preferences for fear of being reversed by the courts above. Segal and Spaeth argue that if justices wish to avoid reversal, and it is assumed of course that they do, then they would be unwilling to contravene the decisions of those courts, deferring to precedent of higher courts. They cite the work of Songer[16] to suggest that there is little "overtly non-compliant behavior" from the lower courts.[17] I do not take issue with this aspect of their model, save to say that recent work calls this understanding of the behavior of lower court judges into question.[18]

Last, and most importantly, Segal and Spaeth assert that the primary institutional feature that allows Supreme Court justices to follow their policy preferences in their voting behavior is that they are not directly accountable to the electorate.[19] They acknowledge that state court judges are influenced by public opinion, but there is little evidence to suggest that Supreme Court justices are similarly influenced.[20] The authors also assert that Supreme Court justices rarely need to fear political repercussions. Justices can be impeached, but such instances are quite rare. Congress does have the ability to change the appellate jurisdiction of the Court, but again, this power has rarely been used.[21]

To this point, I have discussed an important vein that runs through the political science literature on judicial decision-making. Classical legal scholars gave way to the legal realists, the realists acceded to the behavioralists, and from the behavioral tradition grew the social/psychological approach of the attitudinalists. However, the attitudinal approach was not the only strain of thought that emerged from these theorists. *The Roosevelt Court* also spawned a line of thinking that, though it has progressed in fits and starts, appears to have gained substantial acceptance from many in the field of judicial politics: the strategic model. In the following section, I discuss the evolution of the strategic model from the behavioral tradition, how it differs from the attitudinal model, and why it is the most appropriate model to explain judicial decision making. Specifically, while the majority of work conducted by judicial scholars has focused on the Supreme Court, I discuss some of the research done by scholars of decision making on lower courts, and argue that the strategic model is quite appropriate for examining decision making at that level as well.

## Strategic Accounts of Judicial Behavior

Judges play a vital role in the policy making process. Numerous scholars have employed strategic accounts to explain judicial behavior by justices on the United States Supreme Court.[22] and on state supreme courts.[23] These accounts suggest that justices are goal oriented and recognize that the attainment of their goals, whatever they may be, are dependent on the preferences of other actors and what actions they expect those actors to take. Further, the decisions justices make are constrained by the institutional context. In the sections that follow, I outline the strategic model and discuss how it has developed through the work of a number of noteworthy scholars. I then adapt the strategic model to state supreme court justices, for even though it is a highly plausible and credible model of decision making for Supreme Court justices, I argue that it is even more appropriate for discussing the behavior of state supreme court justices. Finally, I discuss the importance of the institutional context facing state supreme court justices, and why those institutions are important for understanding their behavior.

### *Justices and Goals*

Most adherents to strategic accounts of judicial behavior agree with attitudinalists in at least one important respect. Though the general strategic theory suggests that there are numerous goals to which justices might subscribe, such as further career enhancement,[24] making good policy,[25] and avoiding Supreme Court reversal,[26] as Epstein and Knight suggest, "a major goal of all justices is to see the law—over the long term—reflect their preferred policy positions, and that they will take actions to advance this objective."[27] This comment is directed at Supreme Court justices, but it is a position that other scholars embrace as motivation for state supreme court justices as well.[28] It is a position that I adopt in my approach toward state supreme court justices. Judges are political actors and seek to implement their policy preferences within the constraints placed on them by other actors. Before moving toward a discussion of the strategic model of state supreme court behavior, I discuss the general strategic model in more detail.

While Epstein and Knight make a convincing argument for policy as the main goal of justices, they were not the first to suggest that as a goal or that justices behave strategically.[29] As I stated earlier, in the discussion of the attitudinal model, the issue of justices as policy seekers has been discussed by Frank, Llewellyn, Pritchett, Schubert, Rohde and Spaeth, and Segal and Spaeth.[30] Others who have offered strategic models argue that policy is the primary goal of justices as well.[31]

Perhaps the most comprehensive justification for this assumption about Supreme Court justices is that offered by Lee Epstein and Jack Knight.[32] They argue that policy is a plausible, and dominant, goal for Supreme Court justices from the very beginning of the case selection process. They ask the question: If justices are policy seekers, then do they pursue this goal when selecting the cases that are appealed to the Court?[33] As Epstein and Knight suggest, there is at least anecdotal evidence to support such a notion, and likely empirical evidence as well. They cite the comments of Chief Justice Rehnquist who admitted that:

> There is an ideological division on the Court , and each of us has some cases we would like to see granted, and on the contrary some of the other members would not like to see them granted.[34]

H.W. Perry, who conducted interviews with numerous members of the Court, suggests that Rehnquist is not alone in his perception of the certiorari granting process.[35] At least one other justice complemented Rehnquist's perspective by suggesting that, in fact, the likelihood of granting review is increased by the individual's perception that the case was incorrectly decided by the lower court.[36] Epstein and Knight recognize that, though these comments come directly from the justices themselves, they should not be taken as direct evidence that the sole reason the Court accepts cases for review can be directly attributed to the policy preferences of the individual justices.

As Epstein and Knight admit, these data do not serve as proof that justices are motivated primarily by policy concerns when making decisions, but it does provide support for the assumption that justices pursue policy goals. The larger issue at stake is not whether policy is a legitimate goal, but whether it is the primary goal of justices. To address this, it is necessary to go back to some of the justifications that Segal and Spaeth offer for the policy minded justice.[37] A number of factors support the idea that the primary goals of justices is the attainment of policy. These include a lack of ambition for higher office, no electoral accountability, the absence of a higher court to overturn their decisions, that the likelihood of being impeached or having their decisions altered significantly by Congress is small, and perhaps most importantly, that justices enjoy life tenure. All of these factors, combined with the data presented by Epstein and Knight, provide compelling reason to believe that the primary goal of justices is policy.

### *Strategic Behavior*

Justices who wish to see their preferred policy preferences etched into law do not have the luxury of merely voting their sincere policy preferences. That is, justices with even the slightest level of political sophistication understand that they may not be able to achieve those policy preferences simply by voting for their most preferred policy choice. In certain, perhaps most, instances it will be in the justice's best interest to consider the preferences and possible responses of other justices on the court, other institutional actors, and perhaps the public, before making a decision. Strategic behavior can, and often does, take on two distinct aspects: Intra-institutional strategic behavior and inter-institutional behavior. I assume that strategic rationality is most appropriate for understanding the behavior of jurists, particularly state supreme court justices.

These approaches fall into two general categories: Bargaining models, and Separation of Powers (SOP) models. The first category represents those works that focus on the strategic behavior that goes on within the Court itself, among the members. The work of Murphy and Schubert falls into the first category. SOP models generally treat the Court as a unitary actor, focusing on the strategic interactions between the three branches of government. SOP models can be traced to the work of Marks,[38] and have since have been used quite effectively in a number of instances to describe intergovernmental interactions.[39] In the remainder of this section, I discuss the intellectual tradition since the work of Murphy that focuses on intra-court bargaining, and then turn my attention to relevant SOP models.

### *Bargaining Models*

As I said, the early work of Schubert, but especially Murphy, served as the progenitor for the work appearing on bargaining on the Court in recent years. As I discussed earlier, it took a number of years before scholars turned to intra-court dynamics, but now that it has begun, they have done so in increasing numbers.[40] Building on, or at least giving credit to Murphy's *Elements*, the authors make similar claims about justices. They argue that justices are indeed rational actors who must take into account the preferences and possible actions of their colleagues on the bench. Moreover, these studies take Murphy's central assumption to heart:

> Since he shares decision-making authority with eight other judges, the first problem that a policy oriented justice would confront is that of obtaining at least four, and hopefully eight, additional votes for the results he wants and the kinds of opinions he thinks should be written in cases important to his objectives.[41]

In studying the papers of Supreme Court justices, Epstein and Knight find that justices do in fact include statements in their memoranda that involve bargaining issues.[42] Adding to the comments made in memoranda between the justices, justices often make comments about policy implications, lending credence to the assumption that justices are policy oriented. Taken together, the evidence that these scholars find suggests that justices, at least on an internal level, do concern themselves with the policy implications of their decisions and behave strategically in pursuing those objectives.

This conclusion is supported by the work of others. In their analysis of opinion assignments on the Court, Wahlbeck, Spriggs, and Maltzman find that where the majority includes members that are ideologically distant, the greater the activity, or frequency, of comments to the opinion writer suggesting changes before they will join the opinion.[43] Simply put, the greater the disparity in ideology of the justices in the majority, the more bargaining that occurs in crafting an opinion. This finding bolsters Epstein and Knight's analysis. Justices do have policy preferences, and the activity that occurs on the Court suggests that they behave strategically to pursue those preferences.

Though those who study the courts waited for some time between Murphy's *Elements* and Epstein and Knight's *Choices,* we are gaining greater insight into the internal workings of the Supreme Court. In particular, the work shows that justices do engage in bargaining over a number of matters, including the ultimate state of the opinion, and therefore policy. Not only have we seen an increase in the amount of work focusing on the internal workings of the Court and strategic models of behavior in that setting, there is also an active body of work that focuses on the interactions between the Court and the other branches of government.

### *Separation of Powers Models*

The principles of separation of powers and checks and balances that define the workings of our national institutions stem from the framers' fear of tyranny. As a result, each of the branches of government has defined and distinct functions. They also possess the power to check the powers of the others. The *Federalist Papers,* authored principally by James Madison and Alexander Hamilton, discuss in great detail the need for an explicit and formalized system to limit the powers of the federal government, not only through the separation of powers and checks and balances, but also by actually designing a federal system, whereby power is shared between the federal government and its individual units (states). The matter was put quite elegantly by Madison in *Federalist 51,* where he states that the branches of the federal government were designed, and their relationships defined, so that "...the interior structure of the government as that its several constituent parts may, by their mutual relations, be the means of keeping each other in their proper places."[44] Clearly, the Founding Fathers feared the powers of a strong national government and sought to limit the possibility of abuses by designing the system in such a way that each branch has built-in incentive to limit the actions of the other branches. It is this interplay between the branches that forms the basis for the (SOP) models.

As Martin[45] notes, there is a long tradition of scholarly research on the relationship between Congress and the President.[46] However, the Supreme Court was not included in such analyses. As the prestige and power of the Supreme Court increased in the early part of this century, such neglect was not warranted. The Court began to take on issues of greater national importance beginning in the late nineteenth century, continuing throughout the first quarter of the twentieth century. Moreover, the Court was staffed with a number of conservative members willing to use the power associated with the highest court to press their policy preferences. This was aided by the passage of the Judiciary Act of 1925, which gave the Court near total control over its docket.[47] The importance, or more appropriately, the confidence the members had in their power was made clear with their famous battles with the President over New Deal Legislation in the 1930s. Roosevelt eventually won his confrontation with the Court, as members of the Court retreated from their anti-New Deal stances, and with key retirements, Roosevelt was able to place a number of appointments to the Court sympathetic to his agenda.

The importance of the Court as a political institution did not diminish in the post-war years, engaging itself in matters of national public policy including civil rights, criminal procedure, and voting and representation issues. Scholars also began to notice the importance of the Court as a national policy-making institution, and with the publication of C. Herman Pritchett's *The Roosevelt Court* in 1948, the modern era of scholarship on judicial behavior was born. Noting the increase in dissent rates on the Court in the first half of the twentieth century, Pritchett challenged the conventional wisdom that justices merely apply the law and existing precedent, finding that they in fact have policy preferences and that they are willing to pursue those preferences by voicing dissents.

It was Murphy's *Elements,* discussed earlier, that precipitated the move toward strategic models of judicial behavior. While explicitly an analysis of the internal workings of the Court, he discussed the constraints that face the members of the Court, such as public opinion, threshold issues (essentially that the Court is not a self-starter, but must wait for cases to be brought to the Court), as well as political constraints from the other branches of government. He illustrates the interactions between the Court, Congress, and the President.

Interestingly, like the work that focused on the internal bargaining on the Court, it took some time to apply the principles discussed in *Elements* and adapt them to inter-branch interactions. Murphy's work spawned a vein of research that focused on the internal bargaining that takes place on the Court. However, others built on the key tenets of Murphy's analysis of the Court to develop models that incorporated assumptions of strategic behavior on the part of justices, not just in their internal dealings with each other, but also as it applied to their interactions with the other branches of government.[48] These SOP models assumed that justices on the Court behaved strategically, accounting for the preferences of the other branches of government when drafting their opinions, so as to achieve policy as close to their ideal position as possible.

The modern genesis of SOP models is Marks's *A Model of Judicial Influence on Congressional Policymaking.*[49] Following Marks's dissertation, a number of scholars began to model the interactions between the branches.[50]

There have been numerous other SOP applications in the years since Marks's dissertation that have sought not only to improve on the empirical shortcomings of the early SOP models, but to apply them to different contexts to explain policy outcomes. Some have used SOP models to examine interactions between the Court and Congress over constitutional issues,[51] statutory interpretation,[52] and Court/Agency interaction.[53] Others use variants of the SOP models to explain important historical conflicts between the branches[54] and issues involving the interpretation of constitutional liberties.[55] Still others have used sophisticated statistical methodology in conjunction with the SOP model to evaluate strategic behavior in the context of civil rights policy.[56] What all of these studies show, in a number of contexts, is that the Court behaves in a sophisticated manner to achieve its desired policy outcomes when interacting with the other branches. In the following section, I briefly discuss the importance of the institutional context for understanding the behavior of the Supreme Court.

This section started with a discussion of Walter Murphy's *Elements of Judicial Strategy.* It is widely accepted that Murphy's work spawned the work of recent scholars using strategic models of decision making to study the courts. Both bargaining models, which focus on the internal workings of the Court and the interplay that occurs between justices, and the SOP models, which concentrate on the interactions between institutions, can trace their roots back to Murphy. Later scholars have developed increasingly sophisticated theories of behavior, using varying sources of data, to show that justices behave strategically, accounting for the institutional structure. In the sections that follow, I outline a strategic theory of state judicial behavior, in which I argue that institutions are important in understanding the behavior of these actors.

## A STRATEGIC ACCOUNT OF STATE SUPREME COURT JUSTICE BEHAVIOR

All of the preceding discussion has focused on the Supreme Court and the institutional arrangements that constrain justices from pursuing their most preferred policy at all times. Both formal and informal rules structure the interactions among justices on the Court as well as the interactions between the Court and the other branches of government. Though some suggest that because justices serve for life on the Supreme Court, they are able to vote their sincere preferences,[57] the preceding sections suggest that a policy-seeking justice will consider the preferences and possible actions of others on the Court and the other branches in crafting opinions. The discussion of the constraints that formal and informal rules place on members of the Supreme Court was essential for understanding a basic premise of this work: institutions structure the interactions and behavior of state supreme court justices. State supreme court justices are subject to more, and a wider variety of, constraints than Supreme Court justices. I argue that the constraints on state supreme court justices are even more restrictive than those on Supreme Court justices and that this will influence the behavior of state supreme court justices. In the following sections I lay out the primary components of this strategic account of state judicial behavior.

### State Supreme Court Justices and Goals

I build on the argument that I forwarded in Chapter 1, that state supreme court justices are strategic actors. As such, they are going to account for the institutional setting when pursuing both their reelection and policy goals. In laying out a strategic theory of state supreme court judicial behavior, a discussion of the goals of those justices is in order. There are numerous studies of state judicial behavior that have discussed the goals of state supreme court justices, dominant among these being the retention of their seats, and the attainment of policy outcomes in line with their policy preferences.[58]

Other accounts suggest that there are numerous goals to which justices might subscribe, such as further career enhancement,[59] making good policy,[60] and avoiding Supreme Court reversal,[61] but, as Epstein and Knight suggest in their research on U.S. Supreme Court justices, "justices, in most cases, pursue policy; that is, they want to move the substantive content of law as close as possible to their preferred position."[62] This comment is directed at Supreme Court justices, but it is a position that other scholars embrace as motivation for state supreme court justices as well.[63] Judges are critical members of the policy-making process, and contrary to the theory forwarded by legal positivists, judges do not disregard their policy preferences when deciding cases. In fact, as Shepsle and Bonchek suggest, it may be more conceptually useful for us to think of judges as "legislators in robes" pursuing their own policy goals.[64] I adopt this position in my approach toward state supreme court justices. Judges are political actors and seek to implement their policy preferences within the constraints placed on them by other actors.

There is a substantial body of literature on state supreme court justice behavior that suggests that they are influenced by their electoral situation and will likely view the retention of their seat as an important goal.[65] In this regard state supreme court justices differ substantially from federal judges. Justices on the federal level, serving for life, in times of good behavior, would appear little concerned about being removed from office. Not so with state supreme court justices, who must regularly face the voters.

While state supreme court justices are rarely defeated in reelection bids as a result of their actions on the bench, those that face competitive elections may be more vulnerable than their counterparts in states that employ retention elections.[66] As a result of this electoral connection, justices on state supreme courts whose preferences are unpopular may act in a sophisticated fashion to engender less opposition in the next election.[67]

Scholars have demonstrated the importance of institutional electoral arrangements on the behavior of elected officials in Congress.[68] Specifically, Mayhew argues that members of Congress are single-minded seekers of reelection.[69] Fenno recognizes the creation of good public policy as a motivation for members of Congress, while at the same time acknowledging the importance of reelection considerations. He goes further, suggesting that members of Congress weigh the creation of policy against the possible electoral consequences of such action.[70] As a result of these electoral concerns, members of Congress pursue strategies that will increase the likelihood that they will be reelected. For example, Mayhew argues that members of Congress claim credit for their accomplishments and take positions on issues important to their constituency.[71] Despite motivation to create good policy by members of Congress, both Mayhew and Fenno recognize that reelection concerns are of primary importance.

Like members of Congress, state supreme court justices must first be reelected in order to see the law reflect their policy positions. Moreover, though members of Congress and state supreme court justices enjoy high reelection rates, scholars have argued that these public officials are often concerned about voter reprisal.[72] In fact, Jacobson suggests that no matter how safe the seats of incumbent members of Congress, they continue to behave in ways that suggest that they are concerned about electoral defeat.[73] Similarly, Mann argues that despite the advantages associated with incumbency, members of Congress experience "a pervasive sense of electoral insecurity."[74]

These electoral concerns appear to be shared by state supreme court justices.[75] Though state supreme court justices do not often lose elections, evidence suggests that, in several states, judicial elections are indeed competitive, with narrow margins of victory for incumbents.[76] The defeat of Rose Bird, Chief Justice of the California Supreme Court, and two associate judges, is a clear indication of the potential threat of an aroused electorate.[77] However, it should be understood that the defeat of the California justices came only after a prolonged record of voting by Bird holding the death penalty unconstitutional, clearly at odds with public opinion. Her voting, along with that of other liberal members of the court, led to a vigorous, and ultimately successful, effort by pro-death penalty groups to have them removed. Though the fate of the California justices is somewhat unique, Glick and Emmert suggest that we should expect the behavior of state supreme court justices to reflect the preferences of citizens and the elected elite of their state.[78] When members of state supreme courts choose to decide cases counter to the preferences of the electorate and other elites, they may find that such behavior has its limits, particularly in issue areas that are highly salient to the public.

The above discussion suggests that justices may have multiple goals, but for state supreme court justices two goals are clearly of paramount interest: reelection and policy. As the discussion in the previous section makes clear, policy makers cannot achieve their policy goals unless they are reelected.[79] Similarly, state supreme court justices cannot achieve their policy goals if they are not reelected to the bench. The question then becomes one of attainment: How do they achieve these goals?

In order to reach these goals, they must account for the preferences and possible actions of other actors, including their colleagues on the court, the state legislature, the governor, the bureaucracy, and the public.[80] In addition, they must make determinations about the likelihood that any of their decisions will be appealed to, and subsequently heard by, the Supreme Court.

The idea that justices take into account the views of their colleagues on the bench is not new. Scholars have demonstrated that intra-court considerations do indeed occur, at least for United States Supreme Court Justices,[81] but there is no reason why we would not expect the same considerations on state supreme courts and other collegial courts. If state supreme court justices wish to create efficacious policy, they must consider whether their opinion will attract the necessary votes to garner a majority and, as a result, are not always free to draft opinions that reflect their true policy position.

To achieve their desired policy outcomes, state supreme court justices must also make calculations about the preferences of various political actors, such as the governor and state legislature, and the possible actions they might take in response to opinions from the court. I argue that state supreme court justices will be concerned about maintaining positive relationships with other branches out of concern for whether those actors will adhere to, and enforce, the court's decisions.[82] State supreme court justices must also be aware of the preferences and possible actions of members of the Supreme Court. Clearly, within such a system of interdependent powers and responsibilities, state supreme court justices must account for the preferences and possible actions of other institutional actors if they wish to achieve their desired policy.

## Institutions as Constraints on State Supreme Court Behavior

Justices on state supreme courts are also constrained by the public as they must face the voters on a regular basis.[83] Research suggests that though state judicial elections garner little public attention,[84] and the prospects of losing a reelection bid for state supreme court justices is uncommon,[85] the threat of such a possibility may enter into the decision making of justices, particularly on issues that are highly salient to the public.[86] This is consistent with literature suggesting that, though the prospects of defeat are low, incumbent members of Congress still fear the possibility of losing.[87] In some states, state supreme court justices are also constrained by the presence of the ballot initiative and referendum, mechanisms that allow the state legislature and the public to override decisions of the state supreme court. Strategic, policy-oriented justices would presumably welcome information that alerts them to the breadth of public support for particular policies, and the depth of that support as well.

### *Judicial Selection Systems and Decision Making*

According to the strategic account, it is important to understand the institutional context in which state supreme court justices are operating in order to understand the decisions that they make.[88] Institutions are defined as sets of rules that define social interactions in particular ways, and they can be both formal (laws) or informal (norms and conventions).[89]

The focus of this research is on several formal rules. While federal judges enjoy life tenure once they are appointed, state supreme court justices must regularly face reelection. The particular system used by states to reelect justices varies considerably, and it is expected that the differences in reelection or retention methods will have an impact on the behavior of justices and interest groups participating in state supreme courts. While the reelection system used by a state is expected to influence judicial and group behavior, other institutions would also be expected to affect both judicial and group behavior. Specifically, the formal mechanisms that allow state legislators and the public to override decisions of state supreme courts, the ballot initiative and referendum, are expected to affect judicial and group behavior. Justices are not always free to see their preferred policy positions put into law; they must be concerned about the institutional setting in which they operate and behave in such a way as to achieve their goals. Likewise, groups must also be concerned about the institutional environment and tailor the arguments contained in their *amicus* briefs to achieve their goals.

Some suggest that the behavior of state supreme court justices is conditioned by the judicial selection system operating in that state.[90] In discussing the conflict between judicial independence and the desire for electoral accountability, Sheldon and Maule argue that "the various methods by which judges are recruited are either designed to, or inadvertently lead to an enhancement, impediment or a balance between one or the other of the competing demands."[91] The selection system used by a state in choosing, and retaining, its justices should influence the degree of consistency of judicial preferences with the electorate and elected elite in that state.[92] Judicial selection mechanisms should lead to differences in the expected behavior of state supreme court justices insofar as they are accountable to different constituencies.

In particular, scholars posit that justices will be most accountable to the principal actors in the selection process of those justices. In those states where state supreme court justices are chosen by the governor or state legislature, state supreme court justices should be expected to mirror the preferences of those actors.[93] They suggest that patterns of behavior that have been witnessed in appointing justices to the U.S. Supreme Court should be manifest at the state level as well.[94] Governors should behave similarly to the president when appointing justices. As such, "governors tend to appoint persons who have, through their past political, legal or social actions reflected the values, policies and preferences held by governors."[95] Others contend that state supreme court justices elected by state legislatures should behave similarly, responding to the preferences of that institution.[96]

Even greater scholarly attention has been leveled at the impact of partisan, non-partisan, and merit election systems on state level decision making.[97] Inherent in these studies is the assumption that different selection mechanisms lead to differences in the degree to which state supreme court justices are linked with the voters. Actually, that is precisely why the partisan and non-partisan selection systems exist—to provide stronger ties between state supreme court justices and the electorate.[98] This has not gone unnoticed by students of the courts. Baum notes that "it is generally assumed among scholars of judicial recruitment that partisan election of judges... maximizes judicial accountability."[99]

This close connection between the electorate and justices has led some scholars to examine the proximity of that connection in studies of decision making. Hall and Brace have shown that state supreme court justices in six different states are quite sensitive to constituency preferences in death penalty cases,[100] while Hall draws similar conclusions regarding the behavior of Louisiana judges in criminal cases.[101] In general, numerous studies suggest that, at least for issues that are highly salient to the public, or are particularly controversial, there is a close connection between the preferences of the public and the decision making of state supreme court justices.[102]

Recent efforts have been made in numerous states to adopt the merit plan of judicial selection, which incorporates both an appointment and electoral component, purportedly resulting in state supreme court justices that are more independent than justices in any other system, but also, to some degree, accountable to the public. Although this method is intended to make judges less accountable to the public, throughout the 1970s incumbent state supreme court justices regularly received up to 30% negative votes.[103] More recent work on state judicial elections from 1980 through 1995 confirms the conclusions drawn by Baum that partisan election systems result in the most competitive elections.[104] Hall defines highly competitive elections as those won with less than 55% of the vote, finding that partisan elections were the most competitive, followed by retention systems and then non-partisan retention systems. However, as she suggests, the most dramatic indicator of competition—the number of incumbents defeated—provides a stark contrast between selection systems, with twenty-four incumbents losing in partisan election systems, while only thirteen lost in non-partisan systems, and four in merit states.[105]

Hall's findings are supported by even more recent work on the success rate of justices at all levels in merit retention states.[106] Aspin finds that the mean affirmative vote across time dropped from the 1960s through the late 1980s and early 1990s, only to rise sharply in the late 1990s.[107] This decline, from a high of 85.8% in the 1968 elections, to a low of 69.4% in the 1990 elections, however, did not necessarily translate into an increase in the number of judges being defeated, with only fifty-two defeated judges in 4,588 elections, just over 1%. Of those 4,588 elections, over 85% of them were for major trial court judges, and over 90% of the defeated judges were from those courts. Even more striking is that, while just over 30% of the total elections in the study were from Illinois, which requires a 60% affirmative vote for retention, over half of all defeated judges were in that state.[108]

Coupled with the research conducted by Hall, the results are quite striking in this regard; as state supreme court justices become more accountable electorally, the greater the likelihood that they will be engaged in highly competitive elections and are far more likely to ultimately be unseated. As a result, state supreme court justices should be most sensitive to the preferences of their constituency in partisan and non-partisan election systems and far less so in merit retention systems.

### *The Ballot Initiative and Overriding Judicial Decisions*

In twenty-three states, citizens can directly initiate and approve laws and amendments to state constitutions, while that right is reserved only for elected representatives in the other twenty-seven states. I have already discussed why we should expect state supreme court justices to adjust their behavior depending on the selection system in their state. State supreme court justices should also be expected to alter their behavior in light of the possibility that their decisions will be overturned in the form of constitutional amendments.

Research has found that in states with popular initiatives, the behavior of state legislators is affected, resulting in strategic behavior on their part, in anticipation of responses by the public.[109] Others have found that state supreme court justices, like state legislators, alter their behavior in significant ways in states where the public plays a direct role in the policy-making process through the initiative.[110] I have suggested that state supreme court justices are strategic actors and will behave in ways that reflect their concern about the ability of external actors to alter the ultimate state of the law. As a result, in order to avoid their least preferred policy outcome, state supreme court justices will make determinations about the possibility that their decision, or set of decisions, will lead to an initiative effort by the public.

State legislatures and the governor have the ability to temper the decisions of the court through the legislative initiative or referendum process. There is substantial variation in the ability of legislatures and governors to amend state constitutions to undo, or at least alter substantially, the decisions of the state supreme court.[111] Consequently, the threat from these quarters is less in some states than others, as some require a two-thirds vote by the state legislature, where others insist on only a simple majority. Obviously, in such states it is easier for legislatures to exercise this check against a rogue decision by the state supreme court. The initiative, whether in the hands of the public or, less often, wielded by the legislature, stands as a mechanism with the potential to be used by these actors to amend the decisions of the court. It is plausible then to assume that state supreme court justices, when coming to decisions, make calculations about the possibility that their decisions will elicit responses in the form of initiatives to overturn the court's decisions.

## The Importance of Information and the Role of *Amicus Curiae* Briefs

As the preceding discussion should make quite clear, information is crucial for state supreme court justices interested in electoral success and the advancement of their policy goals. In order to achieve their most preferred policy, justices must be aware of the preferences and possible actions of other actors. Information about the preferences of those actors allows the justices to make decisions regarding the possible impact and efficacy of the decisions they make. They must also have information regarding the likelihood that any given decision, or set of decisions, will have negative electoral consequences. Thus, strategic, policy-minded justices must make use of information that alerts them to the preferences of others.

Justices can obtain information about the preferences and likely actions of these actors from several sources. The first is the information provided by the media.[112] It is difficult to argue that state supreme court justices, many of whom are politically active, do not pay attention to information from many of the same sources as most members of society, including television, radio, and newspapers. State supreme court justices also gain information from their own professional interactions with other branches of the government, such as when state attorneys general participate or members of the state legislature are involved as litigants or *amici*. In some cases, they may also be aware of the preferences of the other branches through personal interaction with members of those branches. State supreme court justices are also able to form opinions about the general ideological position of the other branches based on their knowledge of the outcome of elections for those branches. However, the two most important and direct sources of information relevant to the decision making of justices is the information that they obtain directly from the briefs filed by the litigants in a case and *amici curiae*.

### *Litigant Briefs*

The primary source of information for state supreme court justices is the information contained in the briefs filed by the direct parties involved in a case. Epstein and Kobylka argue that changes in legal doctrine are conditioned, in large part, by the arguments made by the litigants in a case.[113] There are numerous factors that influence the course of judicial outcomes and the course of change in the law, including the preferences of the justices, and the attitudes and possible actions of the public and governmental actors, but Epstein and Kobylka argue that the primary motive force driving the direction of legal change is the arguments made by litigants.[114] They evaluate the course of legal change in two important and highly salient policy domains: abortion and the death penalty. By focusing specifically on the briefs filed by the litigants (and *amici*) in cases over time, they are able to demonstrate how the law changed in those two areas.

In addition to the work of Epstein and Kobylka, Wahlbeck further demonstrates that justices are not entirely free to come to their most preferred decisions in a case.[115] Analyzing data from search and seizure cases, he finds that justices are constrained by case facts, existing precedent, and the arguments forwarded by the litigants. Consistent with Epstein and Kobylka's work, the decisions of the Court are influenced by policy considerations, and the state of the law is a non-trivial component in explaining policy change.

What this discussion suggests is that the briefs filed by the direct litigants is an important factor in understanding the decision-making of judges. This conclusion is not particularly surprising or controversial. In fact, there are legal institutions, *sua sponte* in particular, that serve to limit the ability of justices to make decisions outside the bounds of the legal arguments provided by the participants in a case. Epstein, Segal and Johnson, show that *sua sponte* does indeed serve to limit the Court from addressing issues beyond those presented to them.[116] This is not to suggest that justices do not engage in *dicta*, but that there are norms and rules that do exist to limit them from addressing issues not properly before the Court.

### Amicus Curiae *Briefs*

Another potential source of information for state supreme court justices are the *amicus curiae* briefs filed by interested third parties. As Epstein notes, *amicus* filings at the state level have increased in absolute numbers in the past thirty years with a wider range of interests represented.[117] This growth in participation suggests that interest groups view state supreme courts as increasingly important venues for the establishment of policy. As a result, state supreme court justices may be better informed about the implications of their decisions, and of the preferences of other actors, assisting them in achieving favorable policy and pursuing reelection.

Scholars have addressed the importance of these actors and their participation in the courts.[118] Much of this research focuses on the importance of *amici curiae* and the information that they provide to justices, both at the certiorari and merit stages. Caldeira and Wright argue that "*amicus curiae* participation by organized interests provides information, or signals—otherwise largely unavailable—about the political, social, and economic significance of cases."[119] They demonstrate that *amicus* participation in the certiorari stage increases the likelihood that the Court will accept a case for review. When participating as *amici*, groups, as well as other actors, are able to communicate to the justices information about the array of interests involved in the litigation, signaling to the Court the importance of the case.[120] However, the focus of Caldeira and Wright is on the signals that *amicus* participation provides to justices but says little about the information contained in the briefs themselves.

Others have chosen to focus their attention on the importance of *amicus* briefs filed on the merits. Much of this work outlines the importance of *amici* in conveying information in addition to the signaling information that the presence of a brief suggests. Here the focus is on the body—the specific arguments contained in the briefs. *Amici curiae* provide several types of information to justices.[121] These briefs can inform justices about the specific substantive concerns that particular constituencies have regarding the case and its potential outcomes.[122] In their discussion of *amici curiae* participation before the Supreme Court, Epstein and Knight argue that briefs can be particularly relevant when received from parties that have stature before the Court, including the Solicitor General and members of Congress.[123] Participation as *amicus curiae* is voluntary, and when these actors become involved, the briefs serve as a relatively reliable indicator of the preferences of the other branches of government. Expectations about the participation of state attorneys general and members of state legislatures should stand as similar indicators of the preferences of the other branches of state government. Aside from their substantive content, the identity of the party that filed the brief can also provide information to justices about the array of interests involved in the case.

If we accept that briefs are filed to provide information to justices, we should expect that those briefs filed by interest groups would focus on providing information that would assist justices in attaining policy, and in determining their most preferred policy. This might include information regarding the preferences of other institutional actors, the preferences of segments of the population that the group represents (and perhaps segments of the population that the group purports to represent), and the possible impact of the Court's decision. Groups provide information about the preferences of other interested actors, allowing the justices to develop more well-formed beliefs about the environment in which they are operating, and how their decisions may be received.

This suggests, perhaps implicitly, that *amici* serve to provide unique information to justices on the Court that alerts them to issues not addressed in the briefs of the litigants. Spriggs and Wahlbeck question this assumption, performing content analysis on a sample of briefs, both litigant and *amicus*, filed in the Supreme Court for a single term.[124] They find that while *amici* do provide some new information to the justices, in the majority of instances, the briefs filed by *amici* serve to reiterate the information contained in the briefs of the litigants. Moreover, they conclude that *amicus* briefs are most important to the Court when they *do* reiterate information, rather than providing new information. What this work suggests is that the justices are using the information provided by *amici* as an indicator of the reliability of the information given by the litigants.[125] Whether *amicus* briefs are filed at the certiorari or merits stages, the research points to one inescapable conclusion: information is critical to justices, and the briefs filed by *amici curiae* play a non-trivial role in the decision-making process, at least for Supreme Court justices. The focus of this research is to examine whether such results can be expected to hold for the justices on state high courts as well. Having outlined a theory of state judicial behavior, in the following section I turn my attention to developing a theory of group behavior as *amici curiae* in state supreme courts.

## A STRATEGIC ACCOUNT OF INTEREST GROUP BEHAVIOR

While state judicial behavior is key to this work, so to are the actions of groups participating before those judges. Here, I outline a theory of group behavior as *amici curiae* that focuses on the efforts of groups to obtain policy that benefits their members while at the same time engaging in activity to satisfy their other primary goal of membership maintenance. Having provided a theoretical framework for understanding the behavior of groups when participating as *amici curiae* in state supreme courts, I address the interest group environment of the states.

Even though I argue that several institutional characteristics are central to understanding the behavior of both state supreme court justices and groups, group behavior should also be conditioned on the history, and dynamics, of group development in the state. To wit, interest groups may not behave the same way in Alabama as they do in Michigan for reasons that go beyond any discussion of the institutional differences between those states. As an example, beginning in the 1930s, the NAACP realized that they would not be able to lobby effectively in state legislatures in the South to achieve desegregation in school systems. Consequently, they chose another forum where they felt that their resources would be better allocated in achieving their goals—the courts. This is only one example of a particular group's (and a national one at that) strategy, but it does suggest that not all groups follow similar strategies in pursuing their goals.

Scholars of interest group participation in the political process posit, almost universally, that organized interests play a similar and universal role; regardless of whether they are lobbying legislatures or the courts, they are the transmitters of information to policy makers.[126] Supplying information to political decision makers allows groups to attain their policy and group maintenance goals. One forum in which groups can achieve these goals is through participation as *amicus curiae* in state supreme courts. *Amici* are able to provide information, through the arguments in their briefs, to state supreme court justices about particular issues of law, the preferences of other political actors, and the possible policy implications of the courts' decisions.

I argue that state supreme court justices are strategic actors whose primary goals are the attainment of policy and reelection. The information that groups provide to state supreme court justices, in the form of *amicus curiae* briefs, assists them in obtaining these goals. In what follows, I discuss the goals of interest groups and how they act to achieve those goals through the filing of *amicus* briefs. In particular, the information contained in *amicus curiae* briefs aid groups in achieving the goals of group maintenance and policy attainment.

## Interest Groups and their Goals

One of the primary concerns of the Framers of the Constitution was with controlling the numerous and varied interests that would seek to control the instruments of governance for their own purposes. This was nowhere more evident than in *The Federalist 10,* authored by James Madison. Madison argued that it was essential to design governmental institutions in such a way as to limit what he referred to as "the violence of faction." Factions, as defined by Madison, were understood to be

> a number of citizens, whether amounting to a majority or a minority of the whole, who are united and actuated by some common impulse of passion, or of interest, adversed to the rights of other citizens, or to the permanent and aggregate interests of the community.[127]

For Madison, the solution was the construction of a republic, which, with its various parts and multiple actors, would, by design, prevent the growth of any particular faction. By allowing them to grow freely, Madison theorized that factions would naturally limit each other.

This concept, that the nature of the American political system will allow factions to multiply and thrive, while at the same time preventing the domination of any single faction or group, continues in the writings of Alexis de Tocqueville. In *Democracy in America,* de Tocqueville shows both his fear of, and admiration for, the American experiment. In his travels through this country, he observed that:

> The citizen of the United States is taught from infancy to rely upon his own exertions, in order to resist the evils and the difficulties of life; he looks upon the social authority with an eye of mistrust and anxiety, and he claims its assistance only when he is unable to do without it.[128]

He goes on to suggest that when individuals desire some public good, they form "associations," which congeal and direct the interests of their constituent members. Accepting Madison's premise, de Tocqueville argues that "in countries where associations are free, secret societies are unknown. In America, there are factions, but no conspiracies."[129] His comments imply exactly what Madison had hoped for: that the coming together of individuals to pursue their interests is not quashed; that such "associations" or factions are allowed to thrive, and the very openness of such activity is "good" for public confidence in the system of governance and its continued operation. While people may have an inherent distrust of government, that tendency is limited by forcing the melee over limited goods into the public arena.

While Madison and de Tocqueville were among the first to discuss political associations, or factions, and their ramifications, it is important to have a clear understanding of what is meant by these terms. For the purposes of this work, those terms are treated as synonymous. I consider them equivalent to the following descriptive definitions: organized interest, organized association, pressure group, or interest group. It is necessary to provide a somewhat universal, if incomplete, definition for this family of terms. While others may question such simplification, I do not wish to unnecessarily cloud the crux of my discussion. My preferred term throughout will be to refer to Madison's "factions" as interest groups. Where relevant, I will differentiate specific categories of interest groups, but for now, I will limit myself to this term.

Salisbury defines an interest group as "...an organized association which engages in activity relative to governmental decisions."[130] He differentiates between the understanding of the term offered by both Arthur Bentley[131] and David Truman.[132] For Bentley, the "interest" of a group is the activity in which it is engaged, while it is the shared attitudes that make up the interest. The interest is what the group wants. As Salisbury suggests, the focus of that interest, while the particular objects desired will differ, is to influence the actions of government officials.

Others have refined the definition even more. Petracca argues that groups are "...membership- or nonmembership-based organizations or institutions that engage in activities to seek specific policy or political goals from the state."[133] Again, this is really just a re-conceptualization of the basic definition of the term *interest group*. While the Salisbury and Petracca definitions are slightly different, clearly they both recognize that groups have goals, and the primary goal for them is favorable policy for their membership.

Most research that has discussed group goals has done so within the context of lobbying in Congress. Salisbury and Petracca are not the only ones convinced that groups are interested in securing policy concessions.[134] The particular policy position a group takes can be the result of the leadership acting at the behest of its membership or as a reflection of the preferences of group leadership.[135] However the policy position of a group is determined, a primary objective of virtually all groups is to participate successfully in the policy-making process.

Some argue that considerations other than the attainment of policy can serve as significant motivation for groups.[136] One of these is certainly the continued existence and prosperity of the group itself.[137] It is in the interest of the decision makers and leaders of the group to continue to provide benefits to its members in order to maintain sufficient levels of support, financial and otherwise, to participate in the activities chosen by leaders to best obtain their preferred policies.

### Strategic Behavior by Interest Groups

Interest groups are motivated by policy and group maintenance and they act strategically to attain those goals. They make calculations about the environment in which they are operating and follow strategies that maximize their chances for success.

One way in which groups participate in the policy process is through the acquisition and dissemination of information to the appropriate policy makers. Prior to gathering this information, groups must make decisions about which position to advocate and in which venue to participate.[138] In addition, they must identify who might become involved on a particular issue, which relevant decision makers are involved, and what arguments would be most effective in that situation.[139]

In recent years, groups have come to target courts in their pursuit of favorable policy. There are several ways in which groups participate in the legal system, including direct sponsorship of litigation, but my focus here is on group participation as *amicus curiae.* The primary advantage of *amicus* participation is that groups need not expend the financial and legal resources that they would if they chose to directly sponsor litigation. Participation as *amicus* also allows groups the opportunity to publicize their cause in a highly visible manner. As a result, many groups devote more of their resources to the filing of *amicus* briefs.[140] This allows groups to allocate their resources more efficiently, participating in those forums that offer the greatest opportunity to further their goals.

Participation as *amicus* can benefit groups in attracting and retaining members as well. It is in the interest of groups to demonstrate that they are not only pursuing policy that is of interest to membership, but that they are pursuing it vigorously. Filing *amicus curiae* briefs allows groups to show that they are active and effective. As O'Connor and McFall note "A group has to be able to show its members that their efforts are paying off, and filing *amicus* briefs is the easiest way to do that."[141] Thus, participation as *amicus* can serve to attract new members as well as encourage current members to remain.

## *AMICI CURIAE* AND THE TRANSMISSION OF INFORMATION

The role of information in the lobbying process has long received notice by students of group activity.[142] In particular, recent work addresses the issue of information transmission by interest groups to legislators[143] and courts.[144] Some have described groups as mere providers of information, supplying legislators with bias-free information,[145] while Austen-Smith and Wright argue that legislative lobbying is, in fact "an exercise in strategic information transmission."[146] Wright is even more explicit in his assumption that "... interest groups have both the opportunity and incentive to present information that misleads legislators into thinking that policies are working, or will work, better than they actually are, or that there is greater or less political support for policies than exists in fact and that groups do sometimes deliberately distort information for their own advantage."[147]

In providing information to justices, groups have an incentive to manipulate information to their own advantage, though that is tempered by strategic considerations. In their discussion of *amicus* participation before the Supreme Court, McGuire and Caldeira argue that the repeated interactions between groups and the Court serve to limit the likelihood of misrepresentation as groups develop reputations, thereby lowering monitoring costs for the justices.[148] Much like their involvement at the Supreme Court, as groups participate in state supreme courts as *amici*, state supreme court justices may come to rely on the information that they provide. Therefore, despite incentives that may increase the possibility of misrepresentation, strategic, policy-minded groups are unlikely to pursue such strategies. Moreover, through repeated interactions as *amici*, groups will become more capable providers of information, allowing them to better achieve their goals.

Supplying information to justices through *amicus* briefs serves group goals in several important ways. First, it shows current and potential members that the group is highly professional and participates in sophisticated ways on behalf of its membership. Second, implicit in participation as *amicus*, groups expect that the information that they provide will be read, and relied upon, by the justices. Through the selective transmission of information to justices, advising them of the preferences of other institutional actors, the preferences of the public, as well as pertinent legal arguments, groups are able to promote policy that they favor. They must make determinations about which types of information will be most effective in achieving those policy outcomes within the bounds of the preferences of the justices and the environments in which they operate.

Clearly, information transmission is crucial for interest groups, but when participating in litigation, they are limited in the ways that they can provide information to justices. *Amici* have more freedom to present information that assists them in pursuing their policy and maintenance goals. However, if groups expect to effectively achieve these goals, they must provide information that allows justices to achieve their goals as well.

### Interest Groups and Institutions

When discussing the strategic behavior of interest groups, the argument is similar to strategic explanations of state judicial behavior, with some non-trivial differences. Again, it is critical to understand the institutional context when evaluating the behavior of groups. Distinct from judicial behavior, there are numerous ways that groups can act strategically in the legal system. Groups make choices regarding the venues in which they choose to participate, whether to directly sponsor litigation or to file *amicus* briefs, and what cases to participate in as *amicus*. However, the focus here is on the strategic choices made by groups after they have already decided to participate in state supreme courts as an *amicus*. The question that drives a substantial portion of this research then is: what types of information groups choose to provide in their *amicus curiae* briefs.

In an attempt to understand what information groups include in their briefs, we must examine the institutional setting in which they are operating. Like state supreme court justices, the institutional environment will likely influence the behavior of groups. Groups are not necessarily able to see their policy positions put into law in all circumstances. They must also be concerned about the political setting and respond accordingly. This likely means that groups tailor the arguments in their *amicus* briefs in such a way as to maximize their chances to obtain favorable policy. They may account for the judicial selection mechanisms used in states and whether the public has the opportunity to directly overturn decisions of the state supreme court through the ballot initiative.

The institutional atmosphere may also influence the information provided by *amici* for other reasons. As I stated earlier, groups are also interested in maintaining, or in many cases, increasing, membership levels. There may be instances where groups would not expect that their participation as *amicus* will result in a policy outcome favorable to the group and its membership. In such instances, group goals may still be served through participation as *amicus*. By showing members (and potential members) that they are active in particular forums and in particular policy domains, they may be able to retain current members and attract new members. Success may be less important than an open and active presence on particular issues and in certain arenas. In such instances the types of information provided by *amici* may differ from groups participating because they expect favorable policy as a likely or possible result of their participation. Thus, the institutional setting may have implications for those groups participating as *amicus*.

## CONCLUSION

The focus of this chapter has been on providing an overview of the theoretical foundations for the models of judicial decision making and group behavior that I discuss in Chapters 4 and 5. State supreme court justices, like their counterparts on other courts, are interested in seeing the law reflect their preferred policy positions. However, unlike justices on federal courts, the ability of state supreme court justices to see those preferences through is constrained by the fact that the they must face reelection on a regular basis. Therefore, the theory here diverges significantly from that offered by those who have developed strategic theories to explain the behavior of justices on the Supreme Court. State supreme court justices must concern themselves with the electoral consequences of their decisions, and *amicus curiae* briefs, filed by interested third parties, serve as an important tool in aiding them to learn about the possible policy outcomes of their decisions as well as alerting them to the preferences of those who might impact policy as well as their position on the court.

In summary, I assume that the primary goals of interest groups are: (1) The pursuit of policy and; (2) the retention (and possible addition) of members. There are numerous reasons to believe that groups pursue both strategies, and that one of the many ways that they do that is by participating as *amicus curiae.* In the chapters that follow, these assumptions will guide my analysis of the data collected from litigant and *amicus* briefs.

Another focus was to provide a brief discussion of the character of interest influence in the several states being studied. Groups pursue different strategies and choose to participate in different forums. Though to a lesser extent, I believe that the information provided in this chapter will help to shed some light on not only which groups are most powerful, but also in what forums they might likely pursue policy. Some may be more likely to use the courts than to lobby the legislature and vice versa. This information will help me to make use of the data that are presented and analyzed in the following chapters.

## NOTES

1. David W. Rohde and Harold J. Spaeth. 1976. *Supreme Court Decision Making.* San Francisco: W.H. Freedman; Jeffrey A. Segal and Harold J. Spaeth. 1993. *The Supreme Court and the Attitudinal Model.* Cambridge: Cambridge University Press.

2. Segal and Spaeth, *The Supreme Court and the Attitudinal Model.*

3. Rohde and Spaeth, *Supreme Court Decision Making;* Segal and Spaeth, *The Supreme Court and the Attitudinal Model.*

4. Segal and Spaeth, *The Supreme Court and the Attitudinal Model*, p. 64.

5. Segal and Spaeth, *The Supreme Court and the Attitudinal Model*, p. 65.

6. Oliver Wendell Holmes. 1881. *The Common Law.* Boston: Little Brown, pp. 1–2.

7. See Jerome Frank. 1930. *Law and the Modern Mind.* New York: Coward-McCann.

8. C. Herman Pritchett. 1948. *The Roosevelt Court.* New York: MacMillan.

9. Glendon Schubert. 1965. *The Judicial Mind: The Attitudes and Ideologies of Supreme Court Justices, 1946–1963.* Evanston: Northwestern University Press.

10. Rohde and Spaeth, *Supreme Court Decision Making.*

11. Segal and Spaeth, *The Supreme Court and the Attitudinal Model.*

12. Segal and Spaeth, *The Supreme Court and the Attitudinal Model*, p. 69.

13. Segal and Spaeth, *The Supreme Court and the Attitudinal Model*, p. 69.

14. Perhaps the most well-known example is that of John Jay, the Court's first Chief Justice, who left to become Governor of the state of New York. Since then, other justices have left the Supreme Court for other positions in public office, but it would be difficult to argue that those positions were "higher" offices.

15. Segal and Spaeth, *The Supreme Court and the Attitudinal Model*, p. 71.

16. Donald R. Songer. 1990. "An Overview of Judicial Policymaking in the United States Courts of Appeals." In *The American Courts: A Critical Assessment*, eds. John B. Gates and Charles A. Johnson. Washington, DC: Congressional Quarterly.

17. Segal and Spaeth, *The Supreme Court and the Attitudinal Model*, p.72.

18. Recent work by Comparato, Epstein, and Segal (n.d.) suggests in fact that lower courts do engage in noncompliant behavior, and the degree and frequency of that noncompliance is conditioned on the original vote on the merits and the length of time since the case was decided. For a discussion of compliance by state supreme courts, see Scott A. Comparato and Scott D. McClurg. 2002. "State Supreme Court Compliance with the Supreme Court's Search and Seizure Decisions." Presented at the 2002 Annual Meeting of the Southern Political Science Association. Savannah, GA.

19. Segal and Spaeth, *The Supreme Court and the Attitudinal Model*, p. 70.

20. Segal and Spaeth, *The Supreme Court and the Attitudinal Model*, p. 70. For a discussion of state level judges see James Kuklinski, James and John Stanga. 1979. "Political Participation and Governmental Responsiveness: The Behavior of California Superior Courts." *American Political Science Review* 73:1090–99; James L. Gibson. 1980. "Environmental Constraints on the Behavior of Judges: A Representational Model of Judicial Decision Making." *Law and Society Review* 14: 343–70; Paul Brace and Melinda Gann-Hall. 1990. "Neo-Institutionalism and Dissent in State Supreme Courts." *Journal of Politics* 52: 54–70. For a discussion of federal judges see Michael W. Giles and Thomas G. Walker. 1975. "Judicial Policy-Making and Southern School Segregation." *Journal of Politics* 37 (November): 917–36.

21. The Court has shown a willingness to allow Congress to *expand* its appellate jurisdiction (*Martin v. Hunter's Lessee*, 14 U.S. 304 [1816], and *Cohens v. Virginia*, 19 U.S. 264 [1821]). However, the Court acquiesced to an effort by Congress to *limit* their appellate jurisdiction during the period of Reconstruction immediately following the Civil War, in *Ex Parte McCardle*, 7 Wall. 506 (1869). The Court reversed itself three years later in *United States v. Klein*, 80 U.S. 128 (1872), scolding Congress for attempt-

ing to remove the Court's jurisdiction "as a means to an end." Since *Klein,* Congress has only considered, but never passed, legislation to limit the Court's jurisdiction.

22. Jack Knight and Lee Epstein. 1996. "On the Struggle for Judicial Supremacy." *Law and Society Review* 30 (1): 87–130; Lee Epstein and Jack Knight. 1998. *The Choices Justices Make.* Washington: CQ Press; Lee Epstein and Jack Knight. 1999. "Mapping Out the Strategic Terrain: The Informational Role of *Amici Curiae.*" In *Supreme Court Decision-Making: New Institutional Approaches,* eds. Howard Gillman and Cornell W. Clayton. Chicago: University of Chicago Press; William N. Eskridge, Jr. 1991. "Overriding Supreme Court Statutory Interpretation Decisions." *Yale Law Journal* 101: 331–417. William N. Eskridge, Jr. 1991b. "Reneging on History? Playing the Court/Congress/President Civil Rights Game." *California Law Review* 79: 613–84; John Ferejohn and Barry Weingast. 1992. "The Limitation of Statutes: Strategic Statutory Interpretation." *Georgetown Law Journal* 80: 565–582; Rafael Gely and Pablo Spiller. 1990. "A Rational Choice Theory of Supreme Court Statutory Decisions with Applications to the *State Farm* & *Grove City* Cases." *Journal of Law, Economics and Organization* 6: 263–300.

23. Paul Brace and Melinda Gann-Hall. 1990. "Neo-Institutionalism and Dissent in State Supreme Courts." *Journal of Politics* 52: 54–70; Melinda Gann-Hall, 1987. "Constituent Influence in State Supreme Courts: Conceptual Notes and a Case Study." *The Journal of Politics* 49: 1117–24; Melinda Gann-Hall. 1992. "Electoral Politics and Strategic Voting in State Supreme Courts." *Journal of Politics* 54: 427–46; Melinda Gann-Hall and Paul Brace. 1989. "Order in the Courts: A Neo-Institutional Approach to Judicial Consensus." *Western Political Quarterly* 42: 391–407; Melinda Gann-Hall and Paul Brace. 1992. "Toward an Integrated Model of Judicial Voting Behavior." *American Politics Quarterly* 20: 147–168; Melinda Gann-Hall and Paul Brace. 1994. "The Vicissitudes of Death by Decree: Forces Influencing Capital Punishment Decision Making in State Supreme Courts." *Social Science Quarterly* 75: 136–51; Pablo T. Spiller and Richard G. VandenBergh. 1997. "A Positive Theory of State Supreme Court Decision Making." Paper presented at the 1997 annual meeting of the Midwest Political Science Association, Chicago, IL.

24. Mark A. Cohen. 1992. "The Motives of Judges: Empirical Evidence from Antitrust Sentencing." *International Review of Law and Economics* 12: 13–30; Harold W. Elder. 1987. "Property Rights Structures and Criminal Courts: An Analysis of State Criminal Courts." *International Review of Law and Economics* 7 (June): 21–32.

25. Sheldon Goldman. 1975. "Voting Behavior on U.S. Courts of Appeals Revisited." *American Political Science Review* 69: 491–506.

26. Jeffrey A. Segal, Donald R. Songer, and Charles M. Cameron. 1994. "The Hierarchy of Justice: Testing a Principal-Agent Model of Supreme Court-Circuit Court Interactions." *American Journal of Political Science* 38: 673–696.

27. Epstein and Knight, "Mapping Out the Strategic Terrain," p. 216.

28. Melinda Gann-Hall. 1987. "Constituent Influence in State Supreme Courts: Conceptual Notes and a Case Study." *The Journal of Politics* 49: 1117–24; Melinda Gann-Hall. 1992. "Electoral Politics and Strategic Voting in State Supreme Courts." *Journal of Politics* 54: 427–46; Laura Langer. 2002. *Judicial Review in State Supreme Courts: A Comparative Study.* Albany: State University of New York Press.

29. Epstein and Knight, "Mapping Out the Strategic Terrain."

30. Frank, *Law and the Modern Mind;* Llewellyn, Karl. 1960. *The Common Law Tradition: Deciding Appeals.* Boston: Little, Brown; C. Herman Pritchett. 1948. *The Roo-*

*sevelt Court.* New York: MacMillan; Glendon Schubert. 1965. *The Judicial Mind: The Attitudes and Ideologies of Supreme Court Justices, 1946–1963.* Evanston: Northwestern University Press; David W. Rohde and Harold J. Spaeth. 1976. *Supreme Court Decision Making.* San Francisco: W.H. Freedman; Segal and Spaeth, *The Supreme Court and the Attitudinal Model.*

31. Epstein and Knight, *The Choices Justices Make;* Eskridge, "Overriding Supreme Court Statutory Interpretation Decisions"; Eskridge, "Reneging on History?"; Jeffrey A. Segal. 1997. "Separation-of-Powers Games in the Positive Theory of Congress and the Courts." *American Political Science Review* 91: 28–44.

32. Epstein and Knight, *The Choices Justices Make.*

33. Epstein and Knight, *The Choices Justices Make,* p. 26.

34. Epstein and Knight, *The Choices Justices Make,* p. 26.

35. H.W. Perry, Jr. 1991. *Deciding to Decide: Agenda Setting in the United States Supreme Court.* Cambridge: Harvard University Press.

36. Perry, *Deciding to Decide,* p. 194.

37. Segal and Spaeth, *The Supreme Court and the Attitudinal Model.*

38. Brian A. Marks. 1989. *A Model of Judicial Influence on Congressional Policymaking: Grove City College v. Bell.* Unpublished doctoral dissertation, Washington University, St. Louis.

39. Eskridge, "Overriding Supreme Court Statutory Interpretation Decisions"; Eskridge, "Reneging on History?"; Andrew D. Martin. 1998. *Strategy, and The Separation of Powers.* Unpublished doctoral dissertation, Washington University, St. Louis.

40. Epstein and Knight, *The Choices Justices Make;* Epstein and Knight, "Mapping Out the Strategic Terrain"; Knight and Epstein, "On the Struggle for Judicial Supremacy"; Forrest Maltzman and Paul Wahlbeck. 1996. "Strategic Policy Considerations and Voting Fluidity on the Burger Court." *American Political Science Review* 90 (September): 581–592; Paul J. Wahlbeck, James F. Spriggs II, and Forrest Maltzman. 1998. "Marshalling the Court: Bargaining and Accommodation on the United States Supreme Court." *American Journal of Political Science* 42 (January): 294–315. James F. Spriggs II, Forrest Maltzman, and Paul J. Wahlbeck. 1999. "Bargaining on the U.S. Supreme Court: Justices: Responses to Majority Opinion Drafts." *Journal of Politics* 61 (May): 485–506; Gregory A. Caldeira, John R. Wright, and Christopher Zorn. 1999. "Strategic Voting and Gatekeeping in the Supreme Court." 1999. *Journal of Law, Economics and Organization* 15 (3): 549–72; Timothy R. Johnson. 1998. *Oral Advocacy and the Supreme Court.* Unpublished doctoral dissertation, Washington University, St. Louis.

41. Murphy, *Elements of Judicial Strategy,* p. 37.

42. Epstein and Knight, *The Choices Justices Make.*

43. Wahlbeck, Spriggs II, and Maltzman, "Marshalling the Court."

44. James Madison. 1901. "Federalist #51," in *The Federalist Papers.* New York: M. Walter Dunne Publishers, p. 353.

45. Martin, *Strategy, and The Separation of Powers.*

46. See e.g. Nelson W. Polsby. 1964. *Congress and the Presidency.* Englewood Cliffs, NJ: Prentice-Hall; Aage R. Claussen. 1973. *How Congressmen Decide: A Policy Focus.* New York: St. Martin's Press; Richard E. Neustadt. 1990. *Presidential Power and the Modern Presidents: The Politics of Leadership from Roosevelt to Reagan.* New York: Free Press.

47. The Court has original jurisdiction for a relatively small category of cases, outlined in Article III, Section 2 of the Constitution. Congress has also mandated that there are certain categories of cases that the court must hear, most notably those arising out of the Civil Rights Act of 1964.

48. Marks, *A Model of Judicial Influence on Congressional Policymaking;* Eskridge, Jr. 1991a. "Overriding Supreme Court Statutory Interpretation Decisions."; Eskridge, Jr. 1991b. "Reneging on History?"; Linda R. Cohen and Matthew L. Spitzer. 1994. "Solving the Chevron Puzzle." *Law and Contemporary Problems.* 57 (Spring): 65–110; Pablo T. Spiller and Rafael Gely. 1992. "Congressional Control or Judicial Independence: The Determinants of U.S. Supreme Court Labor Relations Decisions, 1949–1988." *RAND Journal of Economics* 23: 463–92; Jeffrey A. Segal. 1997. "Separation-of-Powers Games in the Positive Theory of Congress and the Courts." *American Political Science Review* 91: 28–44; Martin. *Strategy, and The Separation of Powers.*

49. Marks, *A Model of Judicial Influence on Congressional Policymaking.*

50. Marks, *A Model of Judicial Influence on Congressional Policymaking;* Rafael Gely and Pablo Spiller. 1990. "A Rational Choice Theory of Supreme Court Statutory Decisions with Applications to the *State Farm* & *Grove City* Cases." *Journal of Law, Economics and Organization* 6: 263–300; Spiller and Gely, "Congressional Control or Judicial Independence;" Eskridge, Jr. "Overriding Supreme Court Statutory Interpretation Decisions;" Eskridge, Jr. "Reneging on History?"; Ferejohn and Weingast, "The Limitation of Statutes;" Cohen and Spitzer, "Solving the Chevron Puzzle"; Christina Wolbrecht. 1994. "Separation of Powers, Constitutional Interpretation, and the Free Exercise of Religion: A Formal Model." Washington University Political Science Working Paper; Lee Epstein and Thomas G. Walker. 1995. "The Role of the Supreme Court in American Society: Playing the Reconstruction Game." In *Contemplating Courts,* ed. Lee Epstein. Washington, D.C: CQ Press; Knight and Epstein, "On the Struggle for Judicial Supremacy"; Martin, *Strategy, and The Separation of Powers.*

51. Ferejohn and Weingast, "The Limitation of Statutes."

52. Matthew D. McCubbins, Roger G. Noll, and Barry R. Weingast. 1992. "Positive Canons: The Role of Legislative Bargains in Statutory Interpretation," *Georgetown Law Journal,* February 1992.

53. Spiller and Gely, "Congressional Control or Judicial Independence."

54. Gely and Spiller, "The Political Economy of Supreme Court Constitutional Decisions"; Epstein and Walker, The Role of the Supreme Court in American Society"; Knight and Epstein "On the Struggle for Judicial Supremacy."

55. Wolbrecht, "Separation of Powers."

56. Martin, *Strategy and the Separation of Powers.*

57. Segal and Spaeth, *The Supreme Court and the Attitudinal Model.*

58. Paul Brace and Melinda Gann-Hall. 1990. "Neo-Institutionalism"; Paul Brace and Melinda Gann-Hall. 1995. "Studying Courts Comparatively: The View from The American States." *Political Research Quarterly* 48: 5–29.

59. Mark A. Cohen. 1992. "The Motives of Judges: Empirical Evidence from Antitrust Sentencing." *International Review of Law and Economics* 12: 13–30; Harold W. Elder. 1987. "Property Rights Structures and Criminal Courts: An Analysis of State Criminal Courts." *International Review of Law and Economics* 7 (June): 21–32.

60. Goldman, "Voting Behavior."

61. Segal, Songer, and Cameron, "The Hierarchy of Justice."

62. Epstein and Knight, *The Choices Justices Make,* p. 23.

63. Hall, "Constituent Influence in State Supreme Courts"; Hall, "Electoral Politics and Strategic Voting in State Supreme Courts"; Hall and Brace, "The Vicissitudes of Death by Decree."

64. Kenneth A. Shepsle and Mark Bonchek. 1997. *Analyzing Politics.* New York: Norton, p. 450.

65. Brace and Hall, "Neo-Institutionalism and Dissent in State Supreme Courts"; Brace and Hall, "Studying Courts Comparatively"; Hall, "Constituent Influence in State Supreme Courts"; Hall, "Electoral Politics and Strategic Voting in State Supreme Courts"; Hall and Brace, "Order in the Courts"; Hall and Brace, "Toward an Integrated Model of Judicial Voting Behavior."

66. See Richard A. Watson and Ronald G. Downing. 1969. *The Politics of Bench and Bar: Judicial Selection under the Missouri Nonpartisan Court Plan.* New York: Wiley; William Hall and Larry Aspin. 1987. "What Twenty Years of Judicial Retention Elections Have Taught Us." *Judicature* 70: 340–347.

67. Hall, "Constituent Influence in State Supreme Courts: Conceptual Notes and a Case Study"; Hall, "Electoral Politics and Strategic Voting in State Supreme Courts"; John T. Wold and John H. Culver. 1987. "The Defeat of the California Justices: The Campaign, the Electorate, and the Issue of Judicial Accountability." *Judicature* 70: 348–55.

68. David R. Mayhew. 1974. *Congress: The Electoral Connection.* New Haven, Conn.: Yale University Press; Morris P. Fiorina. 1974. *Representatives, Roll Calls, and Constituencies.* Lexington, Mass.: Lexington Books; Richard Fenno. 1973. *Congressmen in Committees.* Boston: Little, Brown; John W. Kingdon. 1981. *Congressmen's Voting Decisions.* 2d. ed. New York: Harper & Row; Douglas R. Arnold. 1990. *The Logic of Congressional Action.* New Haven: Yale University Press.

69. Mayhew, *Congress: The Electoral Connection.*

70. Fenno, *Congressmen in Committees,* p. 141.

71. Mayhew, *Congress: The Electoral Connection.*

72. Thomas E. Mann. 1978. *Unsafe at Any Margin: Interpreting Congressional Elections.* Washington, DC: American Enterprise Institute for Public Policy Research; Gary C. Jacobson. 1987. "The Marginals Never Vanished: Incumbency and Competition in Elections to the U.S. House of Representatives, 1952–1982." *American Journal of Political Science* 31: 126–141; Hall and Brace, "Order in the Courts;" Hall, "Constituent Influence in State Supreme Courts;" Henry Glick and Craig Emmert. 1987. "Selection Systems and Judicial Characteristics: The Recruitment of State Supreme Court Judges." *Judicature* 70: 4.

73. Jacobson, "The Marginals Never Vanished," p. 138.

74. Mann, *Unsafe at any Margin,* p. 3.

75. Hall, "Constituent Influence in State Supreme Courts."

76. Philip L. Dubois. 1980. *From Bench to Ballot: Judicial Elections and the Quest for Accountability.* Austin: University of Texas Press.

77. John T. Wold and John H. Culver. 1987. "The Defeat of the California Justices: The Campaign, the Electorate, and the Issue of Judicial Accountability." *Judicature* 70: 348–55.

78. Glick and Emmert, "Selection Systems and Judicial Characteristics."

79. Mayhew, *Congress: The Electoral Connection;* Fiorina, *Representatives, Roll Calls, and Constituencies;* Fenno, *Congressmen in Committees;* Kingdon, *Congressmen's Voting Decisions;* Arnold, *The Logic of Congressional Action.*

80. Hall, "Constituent Influence in State Supreme Courts;" Hall, "Electoral Politics and Strategic Voting in State Supreme Courts;" Hall and Brace, "The Vicissitudes of Death by Decree."

81. Murphy, *Elements of Judicial Strategy;* Epstein and Knight, *The Choices Justices Make;* Knight and Epstein, "On the Struggle for Judicial Supremacy."

82. See Epstein and Knight, *The Choices Justices Make;* and Epstein and Knight, "Mapping Out the Strategic Terrain," for discussions of Supreme Court concerns about the preferences of other political actors, including elected members of the other branches of the government. While their discussion focuses on the federal level, I argue that the logic of the argument applies to state political actors as well.

83. Terms vary from six to fourteen years with the exceptions of Rhode Island (life), Massachusetts (to age 70), New Hampshire (to age 70), and New York (to age 70).

84. Kenyon N. Griffin and Michael J. Horan. 1979. "Merit Retention Elections: What Influences the Voters?" *Judicature* 63 (2): 78–88.

85. Lawrence Baum. 1983. "The Electoral Fates of Incumbent Judges in the Ohio Court of Common Pleas." *Judicature* 66: 42–50; Dubois, *From Bench to Ballot;* Melinda Gann-Hall. 2001b. "Voluntary Retirements from State Supreme Courts: Assessing Democratic Pressures to Relinquish the Bench." *Journal of Politics* 63 (4): 1112–40.

86. Hall, "Constituent Influence in State Supreme Courts;" Hall, "Electoral Politics and Strategic Voting in State Supreme Courts;" Hall and Brace, "The Vicissitudes of Death by Decree;" Wold and Culver, "The Defeat of the California Justices."

87. Mayhew, *Congress: The Electoral Connection;* Fiorina, *Representatives, Roll Calls, and Constituencies;* Fenno, *Congressmen in Committees;* Kingdon, *Congressmen's Voting Decisions.*

88. Epstein and Knight, *The Choices Justices Make;* Epstein and Knight, "Mapping Out the Strategic Terrain."

89. Epstein and Knight, *The Choices Justices Make,* p. 17; Jack Knight. 1992. *Institutions and Social Conflict.* New York: Cambridge University Press, pp. 66–80.

90. Paul Brace, Laura Langer, and Melinda Gann Hall. 2000. "Measuring the Preferences of State Supreme Court Judges." *Journal of Politics* 62 (May): 387–413; Charles Sheldon and Linda Maule. 1997. *Choosing Justice: The Recruitment of State and Federal Judges.* Pullman, WA: Washington State University Press; Spiller and Vanden Bergh, "A Positive Theory of State Supreme Court Decision Making."

91. Sheldon and Maule, *Choosing Justice.* p. 19.

92. Brace, Langer, and Hall, "Measuring the Preferences of State Supreme Court Judges."

93. Brace, Langer, and Hall, "Measuring the Preferences of State Supreme Court Judges."

94. See e.g. John R. Schmidhauser. 1964. "The Background Characteristics of United States Supreme Court Justices." In *Judicial Behavior: A Reader in Theory and Research,* Glendon Schubert. Chicago: Rand McNally.

95. Sheldon and Maule, *Choosing Justice,* p. 106.

96. James Brent. 1998. "State Senate Confirmations of Nominees to State Courts of Last Resort, 1980–1998." Paper presented at the Annual Meeting of the Western Political Science Association, Los Angeles, CA.

97. Griffin and Horan, "Merit Retention Elections;" Dubois, *From Bench to Ballot;* Hall and Aspin, "What Twenty Years of Judicial Retention Elections Have

Taught Us"; Hall, "Constituent Influence in State Supreme Courts;" Hall, "Electoral Politics and Strategic Voting in State Supreme Courts;" Melinda Gann-Hall. 1995. "Justices as Representatives: Elections and Judicial Politics in the American States." *American Politics Quarterly* 23: 485–503; Paul Brace and Melinda Gann-Hall. 1997. "The Interplay of Preferences, Case Facts, Context, and Rules in the Politics of Judicial Choice." *Journal of Politics* 59: 1206–1231; Melinda Gann-Hall and Paul Brace. 1996. "Justices' Response to Case Facts: An Interactive Model." *American Politics Quarterly* 24 (2): 237–262.

98. Dubois, *From Bench to Ballot.*

99. Lawrence Baum. 1994. *American Courts.* Boston: Houghton Mifflin. p. 167.

100. Hall and Brace, "The Vicissitudes of Death by Decree;"

101. Hall, "Constituent Influence in State Supreme Courts."

102. Hall, "Constituent Influence in State Supreme Courts;" Hall, "Electoral Politics and Strategic Voting in State Supreme Courts;" Hall, "Justices as Representatives;" Brace and Hall, "The Interplay of Preferences, Case Facts, Context, and Rules in the Politics of Judicial Choice;" Hall and Brace, "Justices' Response to Case Facts."

103. Griffin and Horan, "Merit Retention Elections."

104. See Baum, *American Courts,* and Melinda Gann-Hall. 2001a. "State Supreme Courts in American Democracy: Probing the Myths of Judicial Reform." *American Political Science Review* 95 (2): 315–330.

105. Hall, "State Supreme Courts in American Democracy," pp. 318–319.

106. Larry T. Aspin. 1999. "Trends in Judicial Retention Elections, 1964–1998." *Judicature* 83 (2): 79–81.

107. Aspin, "Trends in Judicial Retention Elections," pp. 79–80.

108. Aspin, "Trends in Judicial Retention Elections," p. 79.

109. Elissabeth R. Gerber. 1996. "Legislative Response to the Threat of Popular Initiatives." *American Journal of Political Science* 40 (1): 99–128.

110. Valerie Hoekstra. 1997. "State Supreme Courts, Policy Making and Popular Initiatives." Paper presented at the 1997 annual meeting of the American Political Science Association, Washington, DC; Laura Langer. 2002. *Judicial Review in State Supreme Courts: A Comparative Study.* Albany: State University of New York Press; Spiller and Vandenbergh, "A Positive Theory of State Supreme Court Decision Making."

111. Donald Lutz. 1994. "Toward a Theory of Constitutional Amendment." *American Political Science Review.* 88: 355–370.

112. Epstein and Knight, "Mapping Out the Strategic Terrain," pp. 220–221.

113. Lee Epstein and Joseph Kobylka. 1992. *The Supreme Court and Legal Change.* Chapel Hill: University of North Carolina Press.

114. Epstein and Kobylka, *The Supreme Court and Legal Change,* p. 8.

115. Paul J. Wahlbeck. 1997. "The Life of the Law: Judicial Politics and Legal Change." *Journal of Politics* 59 (August): 778–802.

116. Lee Epstein, Jeffrey Segal, and Timothy Johnson. 1996. "The Claim of Issue Creation on the U.S. Supreme Court." *American Political Science Review* 34 (4): 845–852.

117. Lee Epstein. 1994. "Exploring the Participation of Organized Interests in State Court Litigation." *Political Research Quarterly* 47: 335–352.

118. Gregory A. Caldeira and John R. Wright. 1988. "Organized Interests and Agenda Setting in the U.S. Supreme Court." *American Political Science Review* 82: 1109–27; Gregory A. Caldeira and John R. Wright. 1990a. "The Discuss List: Organized Interests and Agenda-Setting." *Law and Society Review* 24: 807–36; Gregory A. Caldeira and John R. Wright. 1990b. "*Amici Curiae* Before the Supreme Court: Who Participates, When, and How Much?" *Journal of Politics* 52: 782–806; Epstein and Kobylka, *The Supreme Court and Legal Change;* Donald R. Songer, and Reginald S. Sheehan. 1993. "Interest Group Success in the Courts: *Amicus* Participation in the Supreme Court." *Political Research Quarterly* 46 (2): 339–355; James F. Spriggs II and Paul J. Wahlbeck. 1997. "*Amicus Curiae* and the Role of Information at the Supreme Court." *Political Research Quarterly* 50: 365–386; Epstein and Knight, "Mapping Out the Strategic Terrain."

119. Caldeira and Wright, "Organized Interests and Agenda Setting in the U.S. Supreme Court," p. 1112.

120. Caldeira and Wright, "Organized Interests and Agenda Setting in the U.S. Supreme Court," p. 1123.

121. See Epstein and Knight, "Mapping Out the Strategic Terrain"; Caldeira and Wright, "The Discuss List"; Caldeira and Wright, "*Amici Curiae* Before the Supreme Court"; Lee Epstein. 1993. "Interest Group Litigation During the Rehnquist Court." *Journal of Law & Politics* 9 (Summer): 639–717; Epstein and Kobylka, *The Supreme Court and Legal Change.*

122. *Amicus curiae* briefs can also provide information to justices about the manner in which certain areas of law are being dealt with by other courts. This type of information can be useful to state supreme court justices in that it can let them know whether there are erroneous and conflicting interpretations being made by lower courts, as well as providing cues as to how other state supreme courts have dealt with similar issues.

123. Epstein and Knight, "Mapping Out the Strategic Terrain."

124. Spriggs and Wahlbeck, "*Amicus Curiae* and the Role of Information at the Supreme Court."

125. Spriggs and Wahlbeck, "*Amicus Curiae* and the Role of Information at the Supreme Court," p. 382.

126. David B. Truman. 1951. *The Governmental Process: Political Interests and Public Opinion.* New York: Knopf; Raymond Bauer, Ithiel de Sola Pool, and Anthony Lewis Dexter. 1963. *American Business and Public Policy.* New York: Atherton; John Mark Hansen. 1991. *Gaining Access: Congress and the Farm Lobby, 1919–1981.* Chicago: University of Chicago Press; David Austen-Smith and John R. Wright. 1992. "Competitive Lobbying for a Legislator's Vote." *Social Choice and Welfare* 9: 229–257; David Austen-Smith and John R. Wright. 1994. "Counteractive Lobbying." *American Journal of Political Science* 38: 25–44; David Austen-Smith. 1993. "Information and Influence: Lobbying for Agendas and Votes." *American Journal of Political Science* 37: 799–833; John R. Wright. 1996. *Interest Groups and Congress: Lobbying, Contributions, and Influence.* Boston: Allyn and Bacon; Spriggs and Wahlbeck, "*Amicus Curiae* and the Role of Information at the Supreme Court;" Epstein and Knight, "Mapping Out the Strategic Terrain."

127. Madison, *The Federalist*, p. 63.

128. Alexis de Tocqueville. 1956. *Democracy in America,* ed. Richard D. Heffner. New York: Penguin, p. 95.

129. de Tocqueville, *Democracy in America,* p. 98.

130. Robert H. Salisbury. 1975. "Interest Groups." In *Handbook of Political Science, Vol. 4,* eds. Fred I. Greenstein and Nelson W. Polsby. Reading, Mass.: Addison-Wesley, p. 175.

131. Arthur Bentley. [1908] 1967. *The Process of Government.* Cambridge: Harvard University Press.

132. Truman, *The Governmental Process.*

133. Mark Petracca. 1992. "The Rediscovery of Interest Group Politics." In *The Politics of Interests: Interest Groups Transformed,* ed. Mark P. Petracca. Boulder, CO: Westview Press, p. 7.

134. Laura Langbein. 1986. "Money and Access: Some Empirical Evidence." *Journal of Politics* 48: 1052–62; Kay Lehmann Schlozman and John Tierney. 1986. *Organized Interests and American Democracy.* New York: Harper & Row; John Mark Hansen. 1991. *Gaining Access: Congress and the Farm Lobby, 1919–1981.* Chicago: University of Chicago Press; Jeffrey Birnbaum. 1992. *The Lobbyists.* New York: Times Books; John R. Wright. 1996. *Interest Groups and Congress: Lobbying, Contributions, and Influence.* Boston: Allyn and Bacon.

135. Mancur Olson. 1965. *The Logic of Collective Action.* Cambridge: Harvard University Press.

136. Olson, *The Logic of Collective Action;* Robert H. Salisbury. 1969. "An Exchange Theory of Interest Groups." *Midwest Journal of Political Science* 3:1–32; Robert H. Salisbury. 1990. "The Paradox of Interest Groups in Washington, DC: More Groups and Less Clout." In *The New American Political System,* 2d version, ed. Anthony S. King. Washington, DC: American Enterprise Institute; James Q. Wilson. 1973. *Political Organizations.* New York: Basic Books; Terry Moe. 1980. *The Organization of Interests.* Chicago: University of Chicago Press; Schlozman and Tierney, *Organized Interests and American Democracy;* Jeffrey M. Berry. 1997. *The Interest Group Society,* 3rd. ed. New York: Longman.

137. Olson, *The Logic of Collective Action;* Salisbury, "An Exchange Theory of Interest Groups;" Moe, *The Organization of Interests;* Jack L. Walker. 1983. "The Origins and Maintenance of Interest Groups in America." *American Political Science Review* 77: 390–406.

138. Schlozman and Tierney, *Democracy in America,* p. 150.

139. Salisbury, "The Paradox of Interest Groups in Washington, DC," pp. 225–226.

140. Karen O'Connor and Lee Epstein. 1989. *Public Interest Law Groups.* New York: Greenwood Press.

141. Karen O'Connor and Bryant Scott McFall. 1992. "Conservative Interest Group Litigation in the Reagan Era and Beyond." In *The Politics of Interests: Interest Groups Transformed,* ed. Mark P. Petracca. Boulder, CO: Westview Press, p. 271.

142. Truman, *The Governmental Process;* Lester Milbrath. 1960. "Lobbying as a Communication Process." *Public Opinion Quarterly* 24: 32–53; Bauer, Pool and Dexter, *American Business and Public Policy;* Schlozman and Tierney, *Democracy in America;* Hansen, *Gaining Access;* Berry, *The Interest Group Society.*

143. Austen-Smith and Wright, Competitive Lobbying for a Legislator's Vote;" Austen-Smith and Wright, "Counteractive Lobbying;" Austen-Smith, "Information and Influence;" Wright, *Interest Groups and Congress.*

144. Caldeira and Wright, "Organized Interests and Agenda Setting in the U.S. Supreme Court;" Spriggs and Wahlbeck, "*Amicus Curiae* and the Role of Information at the Supreme Court;" Epstein and Knight, "Mapping Out the Strategic Terrain."

145. Bauer, Pool, and Dexter argue in their influential study of foreign trade legislation in the 1950s that "the lobbyist becomes a service bureau for those congressmen already agreeing with him, rather than an agent of direct persuasion," p. 353.

146. Austen-Smith and Wright, "Competitive Lobbying for a Legislator's Vote," p. 229.

147. Wright, *Interest Groups and Congress*, p. 4; Schlozman and Tierney (1986) and Berry (1997) argue that groups are inclined to persuade legislators of their position, but that they avoid outright misrepresentation.

148. Kevin T. McGuire and Gregory A. Caldeira. 1993. "Lawyers, Organized Interests, and the Law of Obscenity: Agenda Setting in the Supreme Court." *American Political Science Review* 87: 717–726, p. 719.

# CHAPTER 3

# Examining Litigant and *Amicus* Briefs

## INTRODUCTION

In this chapter, I develop a model of group behavior, and offer a number of hypotheses regarding the expected behavior of interest groups and other actors participating as *amici curiae* and litigants in state supreme courts. These hypotheses flow directly from the theoretical discussion of state judicial and group behavior discussed in Chapter 2. After discussing the hypotheses, I turn to a discussion of the data to be used. Those data consist primarily of the arguments contained in the briefs filed by petitioners, respondents, and *amici curiae*. In what follows, I outline the model, lay out the hypotheses, describe what data are necessary for this analysis, how those data were collected, and the coding scheme used. In Chapters 4 and 5, I make use of this data to test strategic models of behavior.

## A COMPARISON OF LITIGANT AND *AMICUS CURIAE* BRIEFS

In this section, I provide a number of hypotheses about the behavior of actors participating both as direct parties to a suit as well as *amici curiae*. I begin with a general discussion of the information contained in litigant and *amicus* briefs, followed by a comparison of the information in the briefs of these actors.

### The Content of Litigant and *Amicus* Briefs

The bulk of the theoretical discussion in this work revolves around the behavior of those participating as *amicus curiae*. However, it would be an incomplete evaluation without a discussion of the behavior of the direct parties to a case. The expectations that I have for *amicus* behavior may or may not hold for the participating litigants. In fact, I submit that status, as a party to a suit, will alter the goals and subsequent behavior of the parties in tangible ways. However, before addressing those expected differences, I begin by discussing a number of the expected similarities between litigants and *amici*.

State supreme courts stand as the highest courts in each state. As such they are the final word on state law, barring an appeal to the U.S. Supreme Court. As such, the cases that are appealed to state supreme courts will have, as their main points of contention, issues of state law. Litigants and *amici* will therefore focus the majority of their attention on state legal issues. In the late 1970s, Justice Brennan encouraged state supreme court justices to rely on their own state constitutions and laws to arrive at liberal conclusions. O'Connor responded by admonishing those same judges not to attempt such a strategy, as the members of the Supreme Court would assume that the state court's decision implicated federal law, unless otherwise noted. Whatever the impact the dialogue between the two justices had on the behavior of state supreme court justices in civil liberties and criminal rights' cases, I expect that litigants and *amici* will make reference to state law more than federal law in their briefs across all cases.

***Hypothesis 1:*** *Litigant and* amicus *briefs will contain more arguments about state statutes and constitutions than federal statutes and the U.S. Constitution.*

Litigants and *amici* should also provide more information about the possible impact on, and preferences of, relevant state institutions than federal institutions. By institutions, I mean those other government actors with the ability to influence the policy of state supreme courts. At the state level, state institutions are the legislature and governor. Federal institutions are Congress and the Supreme Court. Again, this is a rather intuitive expectation, with state actors having greater proximity to the state supreme court than federal institutions, and a greater ability to affect the decisions of their respective courts.

***Hypothesis 2:*** *Litigant and* amicus *briefs will contain more arguments about state institutions than federal institutions.*

### Contrasts in Information

*Amici curiae* are not faced with the same constraints that confront litigants. First, *amici* have the ability to choose the cases in which they wish to participate. Litigants do not have such freedom. They make choices about whether or not to appeal a case to the next level. If they choose not to continue litigating the case, their involvement with that case ends. Conversely, *amici* have the luxury of waiting for the most appropriate cases to advance their policy objectives, and they do not need to be involved from start to finish. Second, *amici* may not have as much at stake in the outcome of a case as the parties litigating. Certainly, the cause or interest forwarded by *amici* could be quite lofty and worthwhile, and the results of a single court decision may affect that cause adversely. However, the very nature of the legal process mandates that the litigant bears the most direct responsibility for carrying out the court's decision. This can, and usually does, have a substantial impact on the litigants, both economically and otherwise. The costs incurred by *amici* in participating in a case are certainly less than those associated with direct sponsorship of litigation, but the outcome of the case could have a substantial impact on *amici* who may have to comply with the ruling. As a result, *amici* will focus on those issues upon which they feel the case will turn.

Litigants, across all states, are going to be less likely to devote as much space to the preferences of other actors and policy consequences. Litigants are expected to address a wider variety of issues in their briefs, but they will be unlikely to address them in as much depth as *amici*. Therefore, I would not expect to find multiple references to policy arguments in litigant briefs where there would likely be multiple policy arguments in *amicus* briefs. Litigants are primarily motivated by their own success, not necessarily making policy that impacts others.

The number and range of arguments that litigants make has implications for the specific arguments they are likely to make. There is a finite amount of space that litigants and *amici* have to make their arguments. They must make choices about the kinds of arguments that they are going to make, and in keeping with my expectation that litigants will address a wider range of issues in their briefs, they will only be able to do so briefly. The conventional wisdom regarding *amicus* participation before the Supreme Court is that *amici* will offer information that the litigants are less likely to provide to the court.[1] In most instances, that is information about the preferences of the public, other government entities, and the policy consequences of the court's decision. Therefore, we should expect that at the state level, *amici* will be even more willing to provide justices with this information. This tendency will be further enhanced, or reduced, depending on the institutional structure of the state. In those states where justices are more accountable to other institutions, *amici* and litigants will make arguments about the preferences of these actors.

***Hypothesis 3:*** Amici curiae *will provide proportionately more arguments per brief about the policy consequences of the court's decisions.*

***Hypothesis 3a:*** Amici curiae *will provide proportionately more arguments per brief about the preferences of other state institutional actors than will litigants.*

While litigants are motivated primarily by their own success, *amici* are likely to be more concerned about broad policy concerns. They may participate in a case because it affords them the proper forum to express their views on broader legal and public policy issues. Since I argue that one of the primary motivations for groups is the attainment of favorable policy, I expect that *amici* will frequently provide information regarding policy issues and the possible implications of particular decisions of the courts. While policy arguments can be, and are, couched in many ways—as legal arguments, discussions about the preferences of other institutional actors, or the legal impact of decisions—I argue that *amici* will offer explicit arguments about policy and the preferences of, or possible impact on, the public. By necessity, litigants are forced to address all of the issues in a case, including precedent with a bearing on the case, and as a result, will include more arguments in their briefs than *amici curiae.*

***Hypothesis 4:*** *Litigant briefs will contain more arguments than* amicus *briefs.*

Not only are there reasons to believe that there will be differences between litigants and *amici*, there are also reasons to expect differences *between* litigants depending on the identity of the litigant. Specifically, the question becomes: will interest groups behave differently than government, businesses, and individuals when participating as litigants? There are confounding factors at work in looking at this issue. The motivations of litigants generally are going to be different from those participating as *amici*. There will also likely be differences in the strategies and goals of groups and other actors participating as litigants. I argue that there will be differences in the way that groups participating as litigants will provide arguments compared with all other actors when participating as litigants. Their status as a group, with responsibilities to a sometimes large and vocal constituency, will result in a broader approach to the legal process, resulting in group behavior as litigant more closely resembling groups participating as *amici* than individuals arguing on their own behalf as litigants.

## The Importance of Institutions and Actors

Institutional differences may also be important for understanding litigant and *amicus* behavior. The identity of the actor participating is also an important factor to consider. The following hypotheses address the expected differences in behavior of litigants and *amici*, based on institutional differences between states and the differences in those actors participating in those states.

For states that have the ballot initiative, litigants and *amici* will be more likely to provide information concerning public preferences and policy than litigants and *amici* participating in states without the ballot initiative. In initiative states, state supreme court justices are likely be more concerned about the preferences of the public and the likelihood that they might choose to pass an initiative to modify the court's decisions. In states that do not have the initiative, justices are expected to be less concerned about the preferences of the public and direct policy concerns.

***Hypothesis 5:*** *When groups participate as litigants and* amici curiae *in states with the ballot initiative, cases will contain more arguments about policy than cases in states without the initiative. However,* amici *are expected to behave more strategically than litigants. As a result,* amici *will provide more policy arguments in their briefs than litigants in states that have the ballot initiative.*

Conversely, in states that do not allow the initiative, litigants and *amici* will provide more information about institutional actors than in ballot initiative states. Where state supreme court justices do not fear the threat from the public, they will be more likely to consider the preferences of institutional actors and the impact that their decisions will have on those actors. As a result, litigants will be more likely to provide that information.

***Hypothesis 6:*** *When groups participate as litigants and* amici *in states without the ballot initiative, cases will contain more arguments about institutional actors than cases filed in states that allow the initiative. Again,* amici *will provide more institutional arguments in their briefs than litigants in states without the initiative.*

## Selection Mechanisms

The two previous hypotheses centered on the role played by the ballot initiative, and its influence on the information provided in briefs. Another important institutional feature is the manner in which state supreme court justices are selected and retained. The following hypotheses focus on the role played by the judicial selection mechanisms used by the various states.

Where state supreme court justices are more directly accountable to the electorate (i.e., partisan, non-partisan, and to a lesser degree, merit election states), they will be more likely to be concerned with the impact that their decisions will have on the electorate. Therefore, *amici* should submit briefs to state supreme court justices with exactly this kind of information. I expect that direct litigants to a case will also be inclined to provide this information, but as the definition of the role for *amici curiae* makes clear, this is the type of information that state supreme court justices should expect from them. The direct parties in a suit should be more concerned with providing the court with the relevant legal issues to help the court decide the case. This does not preclude them from including information in their briefs about the substantive impact on particular segments of the population, but their interests are more narrowly defined to winning the case at hand. Making the most persuasive legal arguments may be more likely to improve their chances for success than providing policy arguments in their briefs. *Amici* exist for the expressed purpose of making that information available to state supreme court justices.

Moreover, groups are more likely to provide this information when participating, particularly as *amici*. Interest groups see participation through the courts as one way for them to advance their policy objectives, where other actors may not be so inclined. For instance, the motivations for participation by government, businesses, and individual actors are likely to be different than for interest groups. First, none of these other actors participates in comparable numbers to interest groups. The exception to this may be governmental actors, but their ability to behave as strategically as interest groups is tempered by the general lack of continuity among members of the government. Changes in administrations will alter the focus and goals of government interests, making it difficult to maintain long term litigation strategies.

Businesses and corporations are also less likely than interest groups to engage in long term litigation as part of a larger strategy for the attainment of policy. If certain policy goals are of interest to a particular business, then they are likely to press their concerns through an organization that represents that industry through lobbying and litigation. Their constituents may be of a wholly different sort, but the goals of the National Association of Home Builders, in a broad theoretical sense, are the same as the Sierra Club. They exist to obtain favorable policy for their members while at the same time maintaining their membership base. Participation in the courts is one way they accomplish this, and that is why it is unlikely that any individual corporation that may have the financial resources to participate in litigation on a regular basis will not likely have the incentive to do so on all matters, choosing instead to lobby the national organization to undertake particular issues on their behalf.

Interest groups are the one set of actors who are expected to use the courts with the most frequency, particularly as *amici curiae*. It is a low-cost way for them to pursue their policy and maintenance goals simultaneously. Interest groups are also the most likely to behave strategically, when compared with governmental actors, businesses, and individuals. Groups pursue policy through repeated interactions with relevant government actors, whether members of legislatures, executive agencies, or the courts. It is through such repeated interactions, and familiarity with the forums in which they are acting, that groups should gain the most knowledge about the strategies that will be most effective in pursuing their goals. This is a non-trivial advantage that they have over individuals and corporations in particular. Those actors do not use the courts to the same degree as groups. Also, they do not have the resources to engage in repeated interactions in the courts. As I mentioned before, governments may have the resources, in terms of legal expertise, but they will likely not engage in proactive use of the courts to achieve policy to the degree that groups do, and will therefore not be as likely to behave as strategically as groups.

One final advantage that groups have over all other actors is their access to information that will be of use to state supreme court justices. It is a truism that information is the stock-in-trade of the lobbyist. Those with the most reliable, complete, and accurate information are likely to receive access to governmental decision makers, particularly legislators, than those with information that is deemed to be of less use to those policy makers. I have discussed the role of lobbyists and interest groups, and their importance as reliable providers of information to legislators, but their role is not much different as information providers to appellate courts at all levels. They serve to supplement the court record, providing information that justices might not otherwise have. This is not limited to legal arguments, but is sure to include information about policy outcomes and the behavior of other branches of government. Interest groups are particularly well suited to provide this information, because they exist, at least in part, to represent the views and policy desires of a particular segment of the population. They should be expected to be experts about the issue area they purport to represent and will be in the best position to provide information to state supreme court justices that will be of use in the decision-making process. Ultimately, groups have the resources, and motivation, to participate in the courts, and to learn what strategies will result in the greatest success for their members. They will behave most strategically when participating as *amici curiae*, but should still be more strategic than other actors, even when participating as litigants as well. This motivates the following hypotheses.

***Hypothesis 7:*** *In states where state supreme court justices are more accountable to the electorate, cases will contain more policy arguments than in states where they are less accountable to the electorate. This will be the case for petitioners, respondents, and* amici.

***Hypothesis 8:*** *When interest groups participate as petitioners and respondents, cases should contain more policy arguments than when other actors participate.*

***Hypothesis 9:*** *When interest groups participate as* amici, *cases should contain more policy arguments than when other actors participate.*

In those states where state supreme court justices are retained by other institutional actors, the governor and state legislature, I expect that state supreme court justices will be more concerned about the preferences of those two institutions. The effect will be more pronounced in those states where justices are chosen by the legislature, as they are the lawmaking body of the state and would be better able to modify the state supreme court's decisions through legislation. Therefore, briefs in these states will contain more information about the preferences of state institutions, and the legislature in particular, than in states that choose justices by other methods.

***Hypothesis 10:*** *In states where state supreme court justices are more accountable to other institutions, cases will contain more arguments about the preferences and possible actions of those institutions than in states where state supreme court justices are more accountable to the electorate. This will be the case for petitioners, respondents, and* amici.

***Hypothesis 11:*** *When interest groups participate as petitioners and respondents, cases should contain more institutional arguments than when other actors participate.*

***Hypothesis 12:*** *When interest groups participate as* amici, *cases should contain more institutional arguments than when other actors participate.*

## THE STATES

To assess these predictions, I draw data from several sources. First, a sample of cases was selected from the seven state supreme courts: Alabama, Colorado, Kansas, Michigan, Wisconsin, New Jersey, and South Carolina. These states were chosen because they use different methods to select and retain state supreme court justices, and differ with respect to public involvement in policy making. The specific institutional features of these states are shown in Table 3.1. The table provides information on the judicial selection mechanisms used, whether the state uses the ballot initiative, whether the state has retention or competitive elections, and the initial and subsequent term lengths for the justices.

There is one state included in this analysis, Alabama, where state supreme court justices are chosen through competitive, partisan elections. In these elections, state supreme court justices run against challengers, which is similar to non-partisan systems. However, in states where state supreme court justices are chosen on partisan ballots, the party identification of the candidates are listed next to their names on the ballot. It has been suggested that judicial elections in partisan elections states are more competitive than elections in non-partisan states, and it is likely that this is due in large part to the fact that the party identification is listed on the ballot in these states.[2]

Alabama does not allow for public participation through the ballot initiative. It was my intention to include two states for each particular selection process, one with the initiative, and one without. This proved to be impractical. There are few states that elect judges via partisan elections, and either due to distance or other problems associated with the collection of data from these states, I was unable to include a partisan election state with the ballot initiative in this analysis.[3] This proved to be a problem for the states that choose their state supreme court justices via gubernatorial selection and legislative elections as well. There are nine states that use the gubernatorial selection method, but none of them also uses the ballot initiative. There are just two states that allow state legislators to vote for state supreme court justices, South Carolina and Virginia, and neither of those states use the ballot initiative.

**Table 3.1**
**State Supreme Court Size and Term Length**

| State | Initiative | Selection Mechanism | Retention Election | Number of Justices | Initial Term Length (in years)* | Subsequent Term Length (in years) |
|---|---|---|---|---|---|---|
| Alabama | No | Partisan | No | 9 | 6 | 6 |
| Colorado | Yes | Merit | Yes | 7 | 2 | 10 |
| Kansas | No | Merit | Yes | 7 | 1 | 6 |
| Michigan | Yes | Non-Partisan | No | 7 | 8 | 8 |
| Wisconsin | No | Non-Partisan | No | 7 | 10 | 10 |
| New Jersey | No | Gubernatorial Appointment | No | 7 | 7 | 7 |
| South Carolina | No | Legislative Appointment | No | 5 | 10 | 10 |

*Justices in merit system states, if appointed to fill an unexpired term, serve a short first term prior to their first retention election. Once retained, they face retention elections on a regular basis.

I include two states that use the non-partisan election system. Both Michigan and Wisconsin retain judges in nonpartisan elections. In these systems, unlike the partisan election states, the party identification of the individual judges is not listed on the ballot. Michigan has the ballot initiative, but Wisconsin does not. Incumbent judges in nonpartisan systems are expected to be slightly less concerned about their electoral security precisely because voters are not provided with the party identification cue that they receive in partisan election states.[4] The ballot initiative is expected to increase the sense of accountability to the electorate insofar as state supreme court justices must be concerned about the possibility of popular initiatives in response to their decisions.

Both Colorado and Kansas use the merit plan to select and retain their state supreme court justices. Under the merit system, justices do not run against challengers, but rely on their own records when facing reelection. Voters are simply provided with the option of retaining or removing the sitting justice from office. It has been shown that this system results in less competitive elections than in partisan and non-partisan elections systems, where justices face challengers.[5] The nexus between voters and state supreme court justices is less compelling, allowing, at least in theory, for more independent justices. Therefore, state supreme court justices in Colorado should be less concerned about the preferences of the public than in competitive election states. Colorado provides for the ballot initiative, tempering that independence to a degree, while Kansas does not use the initiative.

As I mentioned earlier, as with the partisan election state, I was only able to include one state, New Jersey, where state supreme court justices are chosen, and subsequently retained, directly by the governor. There are nine states that employ this system and they are located primarily in the Northeast. Moreover, in Rhode Island, once appointed by the governor, justices serve for life, further limiting the number of states eligible for inclusion. I did not want to include a state where there was no accountability to any other actor, be it the governor, legislature or the public, because I was most interested in the differential impact of institutional constraints on group and judicial behavior. Justices in New Jersey do serve an initial term of seven years, and once re-appointed by the governor, serve to age seventy. New Jersey was also chosen because of the relative ease of access to the data, a factor that I discuss at length in the following section.

South Carolina, Virginia, and Connecticut are the only states where state supreme court justices are elected directly by members of their respective state legislatures. None of the remaining states uses the ballot initiative. There is no theoretical reason for including one state in this analysis over the other two, but I chose South Carolina, largely because of ready access to the necessary data.

## COLLECTING THE DATA

The first task was identifying the data necessary to evaluate my expectations of strategic behavior by groups and state supreme court justices. This meant that first, I needed to identify those cases with *amicus* participation. The sample is drawn from cases decided with full opinion in which at least one *amicus* brief was filed from 1986 to 1995.

Choosing this time period requires some elaboration. As others have demonstrated, *amicus* participation in state supreme courts has continued to increase since the 1960s.[6] However, as Figure 3.1 shows, the most marked increase in *amicus* activity occurred in the late 1980s. Though *amicus* activity has increased substantially over time, across states, there is still substantial variation in the amount of *amicus* participation between states. It is necessary to choose a time period where there is a significant population from which to draw cases.

This period was chosen for other reasons as well. In the late 1970s, in response to what he saw as an increasing conservatism on the Supreme Court, Justice Brennan called on state supreme court justices to rely on their own law in arriving at liberal outcomes if they wished to avoid review by the Supreme Court. In a dissenting opinion in a 1975 Miranda Rights case Brennan argued:

> In light of today's erosion of Miranda standards as a matter of general constitutional law, it is appropriate to observe that no State is precluded by the decision from adhering to higher standards of state law. Each State has power to impose higher standards governing police practices under state law than is required by the Federal Constitution.[7]

He followed up this dissent with an article in the Harvard Law Review, articulating and further expanding his reasoning in *Mosley*. Brennan argued, not that the majority was incorrectly interpreting the Constitution, but that "...decisions of the [Supreme] Court are not, and should not be, dispositive of questions regarding rights guaranteed by counterpart provisions of state law...such decisions are not mechanically applicable to state law issues."[8] Justice Brennan's call to state jurists to rely on state law to come to liberal conclusions and to bypass Supreme Court review may have resulted in more liberal interests turning to state courts to press what they may have seen as an opportunity to further their positions in more sympathetic forums.

In 1983, Justice O'Connor, writing the majority opinion for the Court in *Michigan v. Long*, another Miranda rights case, implied that such a strategy as that suggested by Justice Brennan was not likely to produce its intended results as the Court was going to actively review state supreme court decisions for issues that implicated federal law. O'Connor argued that the Court would assume that a decision does not rest on adequate and

Figure 3.1
*Amicus Curiae* Participation in Fourteen State Supreme Courts, 1965–1990

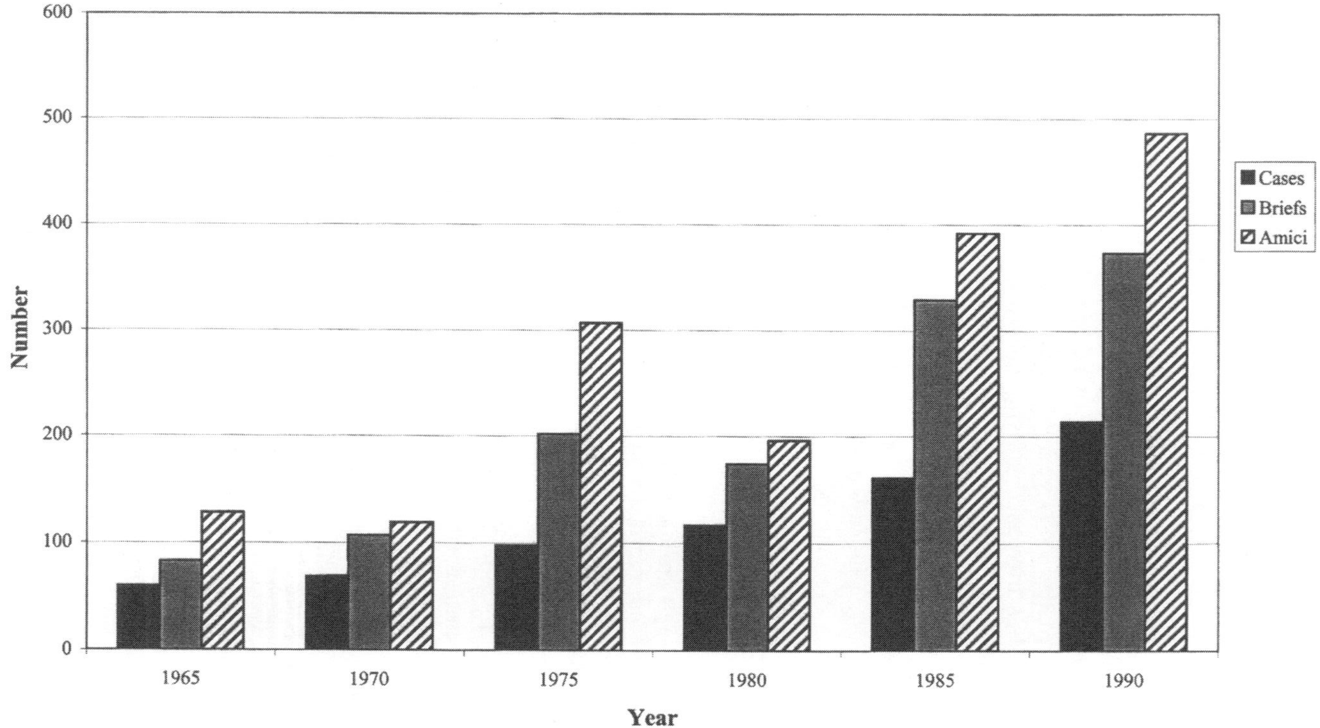


*Source:* Epstein, Lee. 1994. "Exploring the Participation of Organized Interests in State Court Litigation." *Political Research Quarterly* 47: 335–352.

independent state grounds unless the court makes explicit that it relied solely upon its own constitution in arriving at a decision.[9] Whether such advice was followed by state jurists is unclear, but given the large number of cases that the Supreme Court is faced with on its docket, it is unlikely that the Supreme Court would have the time or resources to vigorously pursue such a strategy as threatened by O'Connor. Nor is it entirely clear that state supreme court justices relied on Brennan's advice either. With O'Connor's response in the early 1980s, patterns of participation may have changed substantially, resulting in a decrease in liberal interest participation, an increase in conservative interest participation, or both. It would be most prudent to focus attention on a period beginning several years after O'Connor's statements to avoid the possibility of substantial shifts in the types of interests participating.

After selecting the states to be included, I needed to define the population of cases from which to draw the sample. I made use of the LEXIS electronic database to identify all cases decided with full opinion for the ten-year time period. For each state I conducted the following LEXIS search: AMICUS *or* AMICI *and date (aft 1985 and bef 1996).*

This results in a sample of cases where the words *"amicus"* and *"amici"* are found. However, there are problems with this type of search. First, LEXIS will often provide multiple listings for a case if there is further action by the state supreme court. For example, if a case is held over for rehearing, then there will be another listing in LEXIS for the opinion written by the court in the rehearing of the case. The cites provided by LEXIS were problematic in another sense in that many cases were listed where the words *"amicus"* or *"amici"* might have been mentioned in the body of the opinion, but there was no brief filed in that particular case. Therefore, those cases also had to be identified and removed.

The samples drawn from each state come from populations of different sizes. The number of cases included in the sample represent a range between 5–10% of all cases filed in that state during this decade. The number of cases in the sample with *amicus* participation represents between 12–57% of all cases with *amici*.[10] I would have preferred not to have such a wide range in sample sizes from the states, but ultimately I was constrained by the levels of participation in each state as well as the availability of the data from each of the states.

## CODING OF THE BRIEFS

In order to evaluate the importance of institutions and their influence on information provided by litigants and *amici curiae*, it is necessary to obtain data about the arguments contained in those briefs. As I discussed, I define information as the specific arguments provided by *amici* and litigants in their briefs. Information can be defined in many ways, and it is important for my purposes here to limit the concept to the arguments found in the briefs submitted by petitioners, respondents, and *amici curiae*.

In order to draw conclusions about the effects of institutions on group behavior, I code the *amicus* and litigant briefs for a number of types of information. These are broken down into fourteen distinct categories that may be useful to state supreme court justices in deciding cases. These categories are fully defined in Table 3.2. These data allow me to determine the kinds of information actors provide in their briefs, and by extension, what types of information they believe will be of importance to state supreme court justices.

I traveled to each state to copy portions of the briefs that contained the arguments made in the briefs. It would have been cost prohibitive, and ultimately unnecessary, to copy the entire body of all briefs. The "Cover Page," "Table of Contents" (which includes the arguments), "Table of Authorities," and "Conclusion" of each brief are sufficient to understand the primary arguments made by the actors. I also copied the "Statement of Interest" or "Introduction" when they are present in the brief. By copying these sections of the brief, I am able to discern the arguments made and what legal authority they rely on in making their arguments.

There has been some disagreement over the most appropriate method for coding briefs for the arguments that they contain. Some have argued that researchers should code the "Questions" section of the briefs.[11] This would be problematic for my purposes as the "Questions" section is generally quite short, listing only the main issues to be addressed in the brief. It often does not include particular arguments that the party is advocating.

Others have suggested looking directly to the body of the brief to determine the arguments forwarded by the parties.[12] This would be the most desirable method to use, but it presents a different set of problems. The most serious of these is logistical in nature. This study makes use of almost 1,000 briefs submitted by *amici*, and nearly 1,300 litigant briefs. It would not have been feasible to copy the entire body of all the briefs needed and to then code them for all of the arguments. I simply did not have the time or money to employ this method, given my desire to conduct a cross-state analysis of this type.

Still others have argued for the use of the headings found in the "Arguments" section of each brief.[13] They justify this approach by referencing Supreme Court rule 24.6 requiring briefs to be "logically arranged with proper headings."[14] In his analysis of litigant briefs and oral arguments before the Supreme Court, Johnson proposes a compromise, coding the main headings of the "Arguments" section in the "Index" of the briefs.[15] He argues that these headings are the same, resulting in no discernible differences between his coding method and the Spriggs/Wahlbeck method.

I adopt the coding method advocated by Johnson for several reasons. As I have already said, I was confronted with numerous financial and logisti-

Table 3.2
Categories of Information in Litigant and *Amicus Curiae* Briefs

| Category | Issue | Example(s) of Argument |
|---|---|---|
| **State Constitutional Issues** | Wherever the brief makes specific mention of the State Constitution. Specifically, if the brief makes the argument that an action violates the State Constitution. | Colorado's non-binding court-annexed arbitration system does not violate Article VIII, Section 3 of the Colorado Constitution. – Brief of amicus Richard W. Laugesen in *Firelock, Inc. v. The District Court in and for the 20th Judicial District* (767 P. 2d 1090, 1989). |
| **State Statutory Issues** | Instances where the brief mentions applicability/violation of state statutes. | The District Court erred in concluding that the Colorado Anti-Discrimination Act is the exclusive remedy for victims of discrimination. – Brief of amicus Plaintiff Employment Lawyers Association in *Brooke v. Restaurant Services, Inc.* (906 P. 2d 66, 1995). |
| **State Precedent** | Statements where the party refers to previously decided cases at the state level. Can either be from that state, or from another state. | *Risinger v. Risinger* held that a parent may be required to contribute money to the education of a child over eighteen when, among other factors, the child cannot otherwise go to school. – Brief of ***amicus*** South Carolina State Board of Education in *Washington v. Salisbury* (306 S.E. 2d. 600, 1986).<br><br>*Lee* is consistent with the overwhelming majority of other states which have considered similar limits. –Brief of ***amicus*** Colorado Intergovernmental Risk Sharing Agency, et. al. in *State v. Defoor et. al.* (824 P. 2d 783, 1992).<br><br>Courts in other states, after reviewing this drafting history, have held that the pollution exclusion was intended to exclude intentional pollution only. – Brief filed by ***amicus curiae*** Gelman Sciences, Inc. in *Polkow v. Citizens Insurance Company of America* (476 N.W. 2d 392, 1991). |
| **Federal Constitutional Issues** | Wherever the brief makes specific mention of the Federal Constitution. Specifically, if the brief makes the argument that an action violates the Federal Constitution, then it will be coded. | …violates the Due Process clause of the Fourteenth Amendment by eliminating procedural safeguards and taking property rights of a mortgagee without just compensation. – Brief of ***amicus*** Equitable Life Assurance Society of the United States in *Federal Land Bank of Wichita v. Bott* (732 P. 2d 710, 1987). |

(continued)

Table 3.2
*(continued)*

| | | |
|---|---|---|
| **Federal Statutory Issues** | Instances where the brief mentions applicability/violation of federal statutes. | The federal civil rights statute provides no basis for any damages claim arising from this roadway accident against any individual state employee in his individual capacity. – Brief of appellee filed in *State v. Defoor, et. al.* (824 P. 2d 783, 1992). |
| **Federal Precedent** | Statements where the party refers to previously decided cases from the federal level, specifically the Supreme Court. | This court should adopt "Intermediate" or "Heightened" scrutiny for determination of the equal protection issue under the Colorado Constitution. – Brief of *amicus* the Association of Trial Lawyers of America (ATLA) and the Colorado Trial Lawyers Association (CTLA), in *State v. Defoor, et. al.* (824 P. 2d 783, 1992). |
| **Policy Issues** | Arguments about courses of action the state supreme court should take, or statements about public policy. Includes comments about the possible impact on segments of the population and potential actions those actors may take. This is distinct from the arguments about the preferences of other state and federal institutional actors. | Renewable term coverages benefit the public by promoting accurate pricing of insurance products. – Brief of *amici* American Council of Life Insurance and Blue Cross and Blue Shield of Colorado filed in *Ballow v. Phico Insurance Company* (878 P. 2d 672, 1994). |
| **United States Congress** | Preferences of, and possible responses by, the U.S. Congress to the actions of the state supreme court. | The legislative history of the National Bank Act also demonstrates that Congress did not intend for the term "interest" to include late fees. – Brief of appellant filed in *Copeland v. MBNA America* (907 P. 2d 87, 1995).<br><br>Michigan law comports with congressional intent and requires a knowing, intelligent, and voluntary waiver of rights. – Brief of appellant filed in *Heurtebise v. Reliable Business Computers, Inc.* (549 N.W. 2d 560, 1995). |
| **United States Supreme Court** | Includes arguments that explicitly discuss the preferences of, and possible responses by, the U.S. Supreme Court. Distinct from federal precedent. | The Supreme Court has not interpreted section 85 to require preemption of state contract of consumer law. – Brief of *amici* Trial Lawyers for Public Justice, P.C., and Bankcard Holders of America, Inc. in *Copeland v. MBNA America* (907 P. 2d 672, 1995). |

| **State Legislature** | Preferences of, and possible responses by, the state legislature to the actions of the state supreme court. | The court should defer to the wisdom of the legislature for the determination of appropriate stream usage. – Brief of amicus Kansas Livestock Association filed in *State v. Hays* (883 P. 2d 1093, 1994). |
|---|---|---|
| **Governor** | Preferences of, and possible responses by, the governor to the actions of the state supreme court. | The Governor has interfered with important pollution control programs by impounding appropriated funds. – Brief filed by Wisconsin's Environmental Decade in *State ex. rel. The Wisconsin Senate v. Thompson* (424 N.W. 2d 385, 1988). |
| **State Agency** | Preferences of, and possible responses by, relevant state agencies to the actions of the state supreme court. | The delegation of regulatory authority over the area of oil and gas development to the Colorado Oil and Gas Conservation Commission is constitutional. – Brief of respondent in *Voss v. Lundvall Brothers, et. al.* (830 P. 2d 1061, 1992). |
| **Facts** | Statements regarding the specific facts of the case, mention of the record, and questions of evidence. | The historical development of warrants as means of public finance, uninhibited by section 222 of the constitution, is a product of combined legislative and judicial action. – Brief of amicus Association of County Commissions of Alabama, in *O'Grady v. City of Hoover* (519 So. 2d 1292, 1987). |
| **Procedure** | Issues regarding proper legal procedure. | The trial court erred in refusing to enforce the maximum liability provision of the Kansas Tort Claims Act. – Brief filed by amicus Kansas Association of School Boards in *Kansas State Bank and Trust v. Specialized Transportation Services* (819 P. 2d 587, 1991). |
| **Common Law** | Where the brief makes mention of common law. | Denver's requirement that mountain bell relocate its facilities at the company's expense represents conformity to a long established common law principle. – Brief of petitioner City of Denver in *City and County of Denver v. The Mountain States Telephone and Telegraph Company* (754 P. 2d 1172, 1988). |
| **Threshold Issues** | Arguments about whether the state supreme court should be deciding the case. Issues brought up such as standing, jurisdiction, mootness, ripeness, etc. | The plaintiffs lack of standing to raise the unconstitutionality of voting and office holding restrictions because those restrictions have never been enforced against the plaintiffs and they never will be enforced against the plaintiffs. – Brief of appellant in *City of Birmingham v. Smith* (507 So. 2d 1312, 1987)<br><br>Michigan has jurisdiction to determine the statutory and constitutional rights of one of its citizens. – Brief filed by appellant *in re Clausen* (502 NW 2d 649). |

cal obstacles that precluded using the Epstein et al. approach. For similar reasons, I decided against the Spriggs/Wahlbeck method, realizing that it would entail significantly higher costs because more pages of the actual briefs would have to be copied. Copying the "Arguments" or "Table of Contents" section of the briefs allows me to gain the most information about the arguments offered by *amici* and the litigants, while still allowing a sample of sufficient size to make comparisons across states.

It is important to remember that the previous work focuses on the briefs filed at the United States Supreme Court, while my work uses the briefs filed in state supreme courts, as the main unit of analysis. Therefore, the rules governing *amicus* filings are not necessarily consistent across states. I encountered a number of instances where the *amicus* or litigant briefs were sufficiently short that they did not include a "Table of Contents." In these instances, I copied the entire brief and coded what I considered to be the most important arguments made by the party, as there were no headings in these briefs to be used as a guide.

The primary focus of my research is on the arguments contained in briefs filed by litigants and *amici curiae*. However, I concentrate primarily on the policy and institutional arguments made by litigants and *amici curiae*. More detailed and extensive examples of policy and institutional arguments than shown in Table 3.2 are provided in Table 3.3. The argument made by the American Red Cross, before the South Carolina Supreme Court, is an excellent example of an argument about the preferences and intentions of the South Carolina Legislature:

> The Legislature acted rationally in protecting blood service providers from liability without fault.[16]

The Red Cross is arguing that the State Legislature acted reasonably, and that the court should not use its power to undo their work. This sends a signal to the court, not only about the preferences of a powerful interest group, but also about the competence of state legislators and possible implicit ramifications of judicial interference in the legislative function.[17] Additionally, the following argument, filed in the Alabama Supreme Court by the Alabama Bankers Association, provides an excellent example of a policy argument made by a group:

> The practical ramifications of this decision will negatively affect banking customers throughout the state.[18]

Quite obviously, the association is interested in informing the court of the consequences their decision may have on the public. Presumably, state supreme court justices would be interested in this information, and interest groups are in the best position to provide it to them.

Table 3.3
**Examples of Policy and Institutional Arguments Made in Briefs Filed in State Supreme Courts**

| FOCUS | ISSUE AREA | EXAMPLES FROM BRIEFS |
|---|---|---|
| STATE INSTITUTIONS | References to State Legislature | The Court must defer to the Legislature on changes to the existing discovery rule for medical malpractice actions. – Brief of amicus Wisconsin Hospital Association in *Kohnke v. St. Paul Fire and Marine Insurance Co.* (86-0988, 1988). (Wisconsin)<br><br>The Wisconsin Legislature, in enacting the Equal Access to Justice Act, intended to provide its citizens with the same access to justice in state government as had been provided by the federal government under its Equal Access to Justice Act. – Brief of amicus the Center for Public Representation in *Sheely v. Wisconsin Department of Health and Social Services* (87-2121, 1989). (Wisconsin)<br><br>The legislature's contemporaneous construction of an amendment is entitled to great respect. – Brief of amicus Municipal Association of South Carolina in *Wolper v. City Council of the City of Charleston* (84-CP-10-2111, 1986). (South Carolina)<br><br>The General Assembly has seen fit in the case of fire protection services to protect the municipal investment and to protect the right of county citizens to contract for that service without the county taking unilateral action to interfere. – Brief of amicus Municipal Association of South Carolina in *City of Darlington, et. al. v. Kilgo* (88-803, 1990). (South Carolina) |
| | References to Governor | The Governor has interfered with important pollution control programs by impounding appropriated funds. – Brief of amicus Wisconsin's Environmental Decade in *State ex. rel. The Wisconsin Senate v. Thompson* (87-1750, 1988). (Wisconsin) |

(continued)

**Table 3.3**
*(continued)*

| | | |
|---|---|---|
| | References to State Agencies | The delegation of regulatory authority over the area of oil and gas development to the Colorado Oil and Gas Conservation Commission is constitutional. – Brief of respondent in *Voss v. Lundvall Brothers, et. al.* (91SC169, 1992). (Colorado) |
| **POLICY** | References to Policy Implications | By assuring equal access to family and medical leave, the substitution provision assures that the FMLA achieves the important policy objectives of strengthening families and the workforce at modest cost to employers. – Brief of amicus Center for Public Representation in *Richland School District v. Department of Industry, Labor and Human Relations, Equal Rights Division* (90-1750, 1993). (Wisconsin)<br><br>Public policy considerations relating to the orderly growth and continued viability of municipalities strongly favor reversal. – Brief of amicus League of Wisconsin Municipalities in *Wagner Mobil v. City of Madison* (93-0193, 1995). (Wisconsin)<br><br>The District Court Rulings will disrupt municipal employment relations, create great financial liability for taxpayers, and compromise the ability of government to protect the public. – Brief of amicus League of Kansas Municipalities in *Atteberry v. Ritchie* (87-61066, 1988). (Kansas)<br><br>The court of appeals' decision should be reversed because it is contrary to public policy. – Brief of amicus Colorado Women's Bar Association in *Brooke v. Restaurant Services, Inc.* (94SC312, 1995). (Colorado) |

There were a total of 7,404 distinct arguments made in 994 *amicus* briefs filed in 644 cases decided on the merits. With these data, I am able to determine what issues are emphasized in the briefs, whether there are differences in the types of information provided by different actors, and whether institutional features lead to differences in the arguments contained in the briefs.

## CONCLUSION

The purpose of this chapter has been to provide the reader with an understanding of the primary hypotheses of group behavior, and the data used here. Few studies of the courts have made use of arguments made in briefs for empirical analysis,[19] and an explanation of the procedures in identifying the cases to be included in the analysis, the collection, and coding of the briefs filed by all of the actors, petitioners, respondents and *amici curiae* provides a backdrop for the discussion and analysis of the data in the next two chapters. In Chapter 4, I discuss the arguments found in the litigant and *amicus* briefs in more detail, and develop and test models focusing primarily on the behavior of organized interests. In Chapter 5, I develop a model of decision making based on the strategic theory of state supreme court judicial behavior and test it making use of the data discussed in this chapter as well as additional data gathered on state supreme court justices.

## NOTES

1. James F. Spriggs II and Paul J. Wahlbeck. 1997. "*Amicus Curiae* and the Role of Information at the Supreme Court." *Political Research Quarterly* 50: 365–86.

2. Lawrence Baum. 1983. "The Electoral Fates of Incumbent Judges in the Ohio Court of Common Pleas." *Judicature* 66: 42–50; Melinda Gann-Hall. 2001b. "Voluntary Retirements from State Supreme Courts: Assessing Democratic Pressures to Relinquish the Bench." *Journal of Politics* 63 (4): 1112–40.

3. There are only nine states that use the partisan election system, and of those the majority of states with the initiative are in the far western states, making it difficult from a logistical standpoint to obtain these data.

4. Philip L. Dubois. 1980. *From Bench to Ballot: Judicial Elections and the Quest for Accountability.* Austin: University of Texas Press.

5. Dubois, *From Bench to Ballot;* Hall, "Voluntary Retirements from State Supreme Courts;" Melinda Gann-Hall. 2001a. "State Supreme Courts in American Democracy: Probing the Myths of Judicial Reform." *American Political Science Review* 95 (2): 315–30.

6. Lee Epstein. 1994. "Exploring the Participation of Organized Interests in State Court Litigation." *Political Research Quarterly* 47: 335–52.

7. *Michigan v. Mosley* (423 US 96, 1975).

8. William J. Brennan. 1977. "State Constitutions and the Protection of Individual Rights." *Harvard Law Review* 3: 489–504, p. 502.

9. *Michigan v. Long* (463 US 1032, 1983).

10. In Alabama there were 259 cases with *amicus* participation between 1986 and 1995. 97 cases were drawn from these for analysis resulting in a sample size of approximately 37%. The rest of the sample is as follows: Colorado—103 cases from 323 total for a sample size of 32%; Kansas—103 cases from 180 total for a sample size of 57%; Michigan—77 cases from 658 total for a sample size of 12%; Wisconsin—98 cases from 201 total for a sample size of 49%; New Jersey—96 cases from 341 total for a sample size of 29%; and South Carolina—61 cases from 113 total for a sample size of 54%.

11. Kevin T. McGuire and Barbara Palmer. 1995. "Issue Fluidity on the U.S. Supreme Court." *American Political Science Review* 89 (3): 691–702.

12. Lee Epstein, Jeffrey Segal, and Timothy Johnson. 1996. "The Claim of Issue Creation on the U.S. Supreme Court." *American Political Science Review* 34 (4): 845–852.

13. Spriggs and Wahlbeck, "*Amicus Curiae* and the Role of Information at the Supreme Court."

14. Spriggs and Wahlbeck, "*Amicus Curiae* and the Role of Information at the Supreme Court," p. 370.

15. Timothy Johnson. 1998. *Oral Advocacy and the Supreme Court.* Unpublished doctoral dissertation, Washington University in St. Louis.

16. Brief of the American Red Cross.

17. It also shows how I was able to code the briefs necessary for this research. Only the main heading was coded as an individual argument, and in this case there is only one argument put forward by the *amicus*.

18. Brief of the Alabama Bankers Association.

19. Lee Epstein and Joseph Kobylka. 1992. *The Supreme Court and Legal Change.* Chapel Hill: University of North Carolina Press; Spriggs and Wahlbeck, "*Amicus Curiae* and the Role of Information at the Supreme Court."

# CHAPTER 4

# Litigants, *Amici Curiae*, and Strategic Behavior

## INTRODUCTION

In June of 1975, Robert Carter, a resident of South Carolina, sought permission from the Army Corps of Engineers to make modifications to his property. Carter owned over 600 acres of land near Scott Creek on Edisto Island, of which nearly 400 acres consisted of salt marsh. He intended to fill in approximately five acres of the marsh to create individual lots, which he intended to market as dock sites, priced between $20,000 and $25,000 per lot. During the summer of that year, Carter proceeded to fill portions of the wetland area and sold those lots to private owners, who then added residences and docks to the sites.

The South Carolina Coastal Council intervened to prevent the Corps of Engineers from assuming jurisdiction to complete the filling of these wetlands. The denial of the Corps permit application by the Coastal Council was based on its statutory power to balance ecological and economic interests, and to review any proposed alterations of lands designated as critical.[1] The Coastal Council's creation and purpose reflected what many perceived as an increased awareness and value placed on wetlands. This was fostered by federal legislation in the area, most notably the Federal Water Pollution Control Act (1972), and the Federal Coastal Zone Management Act (1972), upon which the South Carolina Coastal Management Act was based.

I provide this detailed description of the events that triggered *Carter v. South Carolina Coastal Council*,[2] heard by the South Carolina Supreme Court, because this case provides an excellent example of the arguments made by litigants and *amici curiae* in state supreme courts. I argue that institutional mechanisms lead to differences in the arguments that *amici* make in their briefs. In particular, interest groups will demonstrate strategic behavior, where other actors may not be so inclined.

In their brief, the South Carolina Coastal Council focuses almost exclusively on legal arguments. For example, it argues that the trial court judge correctly decided that Coastal Council's denial of the fill permit did not constitute an unconstitutional taking of the property as asserted by Carter, specifically since "... the denial interferes with no existing use of the property and in actuality only precludes one particular type of development of the land ..."[3] The majority of arguments made by Coastal Council address the decision making of the lower court, focusing on technical or specific legal issues upon which the trial court judge ruled. None could be construed to explicitly address public policy or how the decision of the court might be received by other institutions.

The appellant in this case was even more focused on the legal issues central to the case. In his brief, Carter focuses on only two main issues: (1) Whether or not the supreme court has jurisdiction over the case, and (2) Whether the trial court committed reversible error in determining that the Coastal Council was in violation of state statutory provisions. He concluded that the court does not have jurisdiction, and that the trial court did not commit reversible error in rendering its decision.

The single *amicus* in the case, the National Resources Defense Council (NRDC), brought up numerous issues, not confining themselves to procedural questions. The NRDC, unlike the litigants in the case, addressed the legislative intent behind the Coastal Management Act, allocating nearly five pages of their thirty-page brief to the question of legislative intent. They referenced the legislative history of the case, supporting the Coastal Council's decision: "... denial of [Carter's] permit application was based on its general statutory obligations to balance ecological and economic interests and to review through its permitting process any proposed alterations of lands designated as 'critical areas,' here saltwater wetlands."[4] They continued, making a clear and unambiguous policy statement: "The valid public purpose of the restriction which would prevent [Carter's] permanent alteration of his high marsh property should not be defeated by his failure to compromise or to show that, indeed, no value is left to him."[5] The *amicus* in this case is clearly making arguments of a different character than those offered to the court by the litigants. While the Coastal Council and Carter addressed the more formal legal issues of the case, the *amicus* addressed the legislative intent as well as the policy implications.

In South Carolina, where justices are elected by the legislature, and therefore directly accountable to that branch, justices will want information about legislative intent. This will allow the justices to avoid potentially embarrassing, and ultimately electorally damaging, confrontations with the legislature. This is but one example that shows how groups, participating as *amici curiae*, tailor their briefs to present information to justices that the litigants do not. However, the hypotheses in Chapter 3 suggest that this behavior is systematic, with groups making distinct arguments from other actors across states with varying selection mechanisms.

An excellent illustration of the fact that justices in South Carolina may feel ultimately accountable to the legislature is found in the case *Nichols v. State Farm Insurance Company.*[6] Here, while the petitioner and respondent made eight main arguments each, with a particular emphasis on the factual and legal issues of the case, the *amicus* followed a different approach, choosing instead to address the role of the legislature, deferring to the wishes of the legislature, and generally suggesting that the court avoid conflict with that branch. The South Carolina Defense Trial Attorneys Association, participating as *amicus*, made ten separate arguments, three of which made reference to state precedent, one that discussed explicitly the public perception of the court as a liberal body, two that suggested the court ought to defer to the legislature in this instance, and four that involved potential policy consequences of this case. The *amicus* made a strong case in support of competency of the legislature and the proper role of each branch: "A number of questions are involved which can only be resolved by the type of investigation and gathering of facts which is a peculiarly legislative function."[7] The *amicus* went further, suggesting that the court would be overstepping its bounds if it were to decide certain issues relevant to the case: "...it is inappropriate to suggest to this court that it should question the motives, intentions or performance of the General Assembly."[8] Clearly the *amicus* attempted to warn the court away from entangling itself in an issue that the *amicus* believed it should avoid, deferring instead to the legislature.

South Carolina is not the only state in which the behavior of interest groups participating as *amici curiae* is expected to differ from litigants. The focus of *Heurtebise v. Reliable Business Computers, Inc.,*[9] a case brought in Michigan, a non-partisan election state, was on the appropriateness of binding arbitration in workers' compensation claims. The case elicited substantial attention from *amici* with nine briefs filed by various legal, educational, and business-related groups. In this state, where justices are presumably more accountable to the public, there are marked differences in arguments made by the litigants and the *amici*. Heurtebise makes four separate arguments, the first dealing with the matter of the contract between the employer and the employee: "Arbitration is a matter of contract, and the court of appeals clearly erred in finding the arbitration provision enforceable against Ms. Heurtebise."[10] The other three arguments center on errors made by the lower court regarding legal procedure, and non-policy-oriented issues. The respondent makes five arguments, each of them responding in turn to the arguments forwarded by Heurtebise, adding that: "The court of appeals correctly held that the arbitration provision is not ambiguous."[11]

The arguments of the *amici* are distinctive, both in substance and form. The *amicus* brief filed jointly by the Association of Trial Lawyers of America, the Michigan Trial Lawyers Association, and the American Civil Liberties Union, in support of Heurtebise, address only two major points. While they ostensibly address legal issues, the manner in which those arguments are made is quite different from those made by the litigants. The *amici* argued that "Employer mandated arbitration is anathema to employment discrimination claims, which are about obtaining justice and furthering the goals of anti-discrimination legislation, not merely resolving disputes."[12] The *amici* went further, making an even more pointed and emotional argument calling into question the legislation, suggesting that the arbitration process has significant potential impact on the public: "Where the arbitration process is neither fair nor perceived to be fair, as exists in the context of employer mandated arbitration of civil rights and employment discrimination claims, it cannot provide justice."[13] The *amici* were addressing the court in a manner unlike the litigants, couching the issues in quite different terms than those directly involved in the case. This is entirely in keeping with the expected information that *amici* provide generally, providing the courts with policy information that they might not otherwise obtain from the litigants. It is also consistent with the hypotheses in Chapter 4 that interest groups participating as *amici* in states with a more proximate electoral connection to the public will be more likely to make policy arguments to the court, informing them of the potential implications of their decisions on the public.

These anecdotal accounts provide a backdrop for the remainder of this chapter. In the following pages, I concentrate on the arguments made by both the direct parties in a case, and those participating as *amici curiae*. I make clear that the assumptions about the behavior of litigants and *amici* differ in important ways. Individuals, corporations, governmental actors, and interest groups that participate as direct parties in a case rather than through the filing of *amicus* briefs, will likely be pursuing different goals than *amici curiae*. As a result, their behavior, in the form of the construction and presentation of their briefs, will differ from the briefs filed by those same actors when participating as *amici*. Furthermore, I argue that interest groups are different than other actors, and they will behave differently than individuals, businesses, and governments.

In the remainder of this chapter, I analyze those briefs filed by litigants and *amici curiae*. I discuss data on the identity of the litigants and the types of arguments made by those actors. I have a number of expectations about the information provided by litigants, and how that compares with the information contained in the briefs of *amici*. These expectations, formally presented in Chapter 3, are presented in greater detail, and the data on arguments made by litigants and *amici* will be used to evaluate these expectations.

## LITIGANTS AND *AMICI CURIAE:* WHO ARE THEY AND WHAT DO THEY WANT?

Before assessing any particular expectations about the arguments contained in the briefs of litigants and *amici curiae,* I provide a description of the identities of the actors and their substantive interests. In what follows, I sort the litigants and *amici* into categories based on the identity of the actor as well as their substantive interest. I then discuss the distribution of the litigants and *amici* by each set of classifications: their identity and substantive focus.

I separate the actors into four general categories: Businesses and Corporations, Government, Individuals, and Interest Groups. These four categories encompass over ninety-nine percent of all actors participating as petitioners, respondents, and *amici curiae.* All those that could not be classified in one of these four categories were labeled as Other. Those categories and examples of actors in each category are provided in Table 4.1.

The categorization of these actors is worth some discussion. The most significant concern may be may be differentiating between businesses/

**Table 4.1**
**Actor Classification Key**

| Category | Example |
|---|---|
| ***Business/Corporation*** | State Farm Mutual Automobile Insurance Company, Upjohn Company, AT&T, Milwaukee Brewers Baseball Club, Energen Corp. |
| ***Government*** | |
| *State* | South Carolina Coastal Council, Kansas Department of Social Services, Wisconsin Attorney General |
| *City* | City of Colorado Springs, City of Denver |
| *Municipality* | County Tax Assessor, Board of County Commissioners |
| *Other* | Sanitation District, Water Conservancy District, New Jersey Turnpike, United States Army |
| ***Group*** | American Civil Liberties Union, Association of Trial Lawyers of America, Kansas Hospital Association, Farmers Union Cooperative Association |
| ***Individual*** | Robert Carter, Rhonda Heurtebiese |
| ***Other*** | Tract of Land |

corporations and interest groups. Many of the actors participating are professional associations representing certain industries. For example, State Farm Mutual Automobile Insurance Company and the Upjohn Company are coded as individual businesses, but the American Automobile Manufacturers Association and the Kansas Hospital Association are coded as interest groups. Where there is an association or organization that represents a number of individual businesses or professionals, they are coded as groups. This distinction is also important for distinguishing between individuals and groups. An individual attorney or physician is coded as an individual, whereas the Michigan Trial Attorneys Association is coded as an interest group.

Coding government actors presents a different set of problems. First, I divide governmental actors into several different categories based on the level of government: state, city, Municipality, and other. The state and city categories are largely self-explanatory, but by way of example, when the state attorney general participates in any capacity, *amicus* or litigant, they are coded as representing the State. In a number of cases, the governor of the state is named as a party to a suit and is correspondingly coded as a state actor. When a city is represented by their city attorney, then it is coded as a city. Municipalities generally refer to governing bodies that fall between state level government and cities: counties, townships, and other governmental districts. Some governmental entities defy categorization in this manner. These include quasi-governmental units such as sewer districts, utility cooperatives, and localized redevelopment agencies. Other refers to those government interests that do not fall into one of the above four categories, including the federal government, such as when it participates through the U.S. Attorney General.

In addition to the identity of the actors participating, I also code for the substantive *interest* of those actors. These categories are listed in Table 4.2. I define the interest of the participant as the primary function or purpose of that actor. Those categories are more extensive and detailed than the actor classifications. The interests categories are: *Business/Commercial, Government, Health/Medical, Labor, Civil Rights/Liberties, Public Affairs/Good Government, Religious, Legal, Other,* and *Unidentified. Business/Commercial* actors are, nearly by definition, focused on economic/commercial concerns. *Government* refers to those actors whose activities are directed either at the promotion or subsistence of governmental entities. *Health/Medical* refers to those actors whose purpose or profession is the health care industry, which includes individual hospitals, hospital associations, physicians, and organizations of health care workers. *Labor* refers specifically to unions and other organizations representing the interests of workers in a specific industry. The category *Civil Rights/Liberties* covers those individuals, organizations, and associations that focus on the protection and advancement of the Bill of Rights and the rights of minorities and women. Examples of

**Table 4.2**
**Interest Classification Key**

| Category | Example |
|---|---|
| ***Business/Commercial*** | Alabama Catfish Producers Association, American Automobile Manufacturers Association, North American Securities Administrators Association |
| ***Government*** | Kansas Secretary of State, Colorado Municipal League, City of Aurora |
| ***Health/Medical*** | Medical Association of Alabama, Kansas Hospital Association |
| ***Labor*** | AFL-CIO, Farm Workers Association |
| ***Civil Rights/Liberties*** | ACLU of Kansas, Student Press Law Center, NAACP |
| ***Public Affairs/Good Govt.*** | Public Citizen, Michigan Head Injury Alliance, Youth Advocacy Center, Sierra Club |
| ***Religious*** | Catholic League |
| ***Legal*** | Colorado Trial Lawyers Association, Wisconsin Academy of Trial Lawyers |
| ***Other*** | Michigan Bowling Association |
| ***Unidentified*** | One Voice, Foundation Aid District Association |

this category are the National Rifle Association, the American Civil Liberties Union, the National Association for the Advancement of Colored People, and the National Organization for Women. *Public Affairs/Good Government* includes those organizations that are often referred to as "watchdog groups" whose purpose is to monitor the activities not only of government but private industry as well. This category includes groups such as the Sierra Club and Public Citizen. *Religious* actors and their substantive policy interests include groups such as the Christian Coalition, but would also include individual churches and other non-secular actors participating in the courts. The *Legal* category includes a wide variety of actors, including individual attorneys (often involved in disbarment proceedings), and organizations of attorneys such as the Kansas Trial Attorneys Association, or the Michigan Defense Attorneys Association. There are those interests that do not fall into one of these categories and therefore are categorized as

*Other.* These included such organizations as the Michigan Bowling Association and the Michigan Boating Association. Lastly, those participants that could not be readily categorized were classified as *Unidentified.* This category of interest was overwhelmingly comprised of individuals participating as *amici* and litigants.

In the following sections, I describe the actors participating in state supreme courts, and their substantive interests. This discussion is divided into those actors participating as petitioners, respondents, and *amici curiae*. Following the description of those actors, I turn to specific hypotheses regarding the behavior of these actors.

## Petitioners and Respondents

The most notable aspect of those participating as litigants is that individuals constitute a large proportion of all actors participating as petitioners and respondents. However, there are some substantial differences between states as well as whether or not the litigant is a petitioner or respondent. I begin with a discussion of petitioners. Those actors involved as petitioners are outlined in Table 4.3. For petitioners across all states, over 50 percent are individuals. This ranges from a low of 40 percent in Michigan to a high of over 70 percent in Alabama. The second most frequent actors as petitioners are businesses for all states. Though businesses and corporations are the second most frequent participants as a percentage of all petitioners, they are indeed a distant second in most states. The exceptions to this are in Michigan and New Jersey, where businesses make up a sizable percentage of the actors participating at 32 percent and 29 percent respectively. Businesses make up no more 25 percent of the total actors in any of the other states. Government actors are much less often involved as petitioners, ranging from 8 percent of petitioners in Alabama to 27 percent of petitioners in Colorado.

Respondent participation takes on a slightly different character. As Table 4.4 shows, individuals remain the largest category, for all states, and make up 46 percent of all respondents when all states are pooled. Clearly, individuals do not participate as frequently as they do for petitioners. As a percentage of respondents, individuals range from a low of 28 percent in South Carolina to a high of 60 percent in Colorado. Businesses and government actors make up a much larger share of respondents than petitioners. Business interests constitute nearly 28 percent of all respondents in South Carolina rising to a high of 34 percent in New Jersey.

Government participation as respondents approaches the level of participation of businesses, and in three states, surpassing business. State government, the largest percentage of actors in the government category, is involved as respondent in numerous cases, perhaps in part due to the number of prisoners' rights cases that state supreme courts hear. Governmental actors make up the second largest category of participants, over

**Table 4.3**
**Actor Classification, Petitioner**

| | State | | | | | | |
|---|---|---|---|---|---|---|---|
| | *Alabama* | *Colorado* | *Kansas* | *Michigan* | *Wisconsin* | *New Jersey* | *South Carolina* |
| Business/Corporation | 29 | 27 | 38 | 33 | 30 | 41 | 26 |
| Government | | | | | | | |
| State | 6 | 17 | 13 | 12 | 15 | 19 | 8 |
| City | 5 | 14 | 4 | 0 | 2 | 3 | 6 |
| Municipality | 2 | 5 | 4 | 6 | 6 | 4 | 13 |
| Other | 1 | 3 | 1 | 2 | 1 | 6 | 1 |
| Group | 3 | 7 | 5 | 7 | 5 | 7 | 6 |
| Individual | 121 | 73 | 87 | 42 | 75 | 68 | 72 |
| Other | 1 | 0 | 0 | 0 | 5 | 0 | 0 |
| **Total** | 168 | 146 | 152 | 104 | 134 | 148 | 132 |
| **Total Briefs** | 97 | 103 | 103 | 67 | 98 | 96 | 61 |
| **Total Cases** | 97 | 103 | 103 | 67 | 98 | 96 | 61 |

Table 4.4
**Actor Classification, Respondent**

| | State | | | | | | |
|---|---|---|---|---|---|---|---|
| | *Alabama* | *Colorado* | *Kansas* | *Michigan* | *Wisconsin* | *New Jersey* | *South Carolina* |
| Business/Corporation | 50 | 52 | 61 | 32 | 42 | 41 | 27 |
| Government | | | | | | | |
| State | 7 | 25 | 24 | 14 | 15 | 5 | 18 |
| City | 12 | 11 | 7 | 1 | 14 | 1 | 13 |
| Municipality | 10 | 13 | 4 | 10 | 15 | 14 | 6 |
| Other | 0 | 1 | 1 | 0 | 0 | 2 | 1 |
| Group | 5 | 4 | 5 | 2 | 1 | 4 | 4 |
| Individual | 66 | 161 | 65 | 60 | 72 | 52 | 28 |
| Other | 0 | 0 | 0 | 0 | 3 | 0 | 0 |
| **Total** | 150 | 267 | 167 | 119 | 162 | 121 | 97 |
| **Total Briefs** | 97 | 103 | 103 | 67 | 98 | 96 | 61 |
| **Total Cases** | 97 | 103 | 103 | 67 | 98 | 96 | 61 |

businesses, in South Carolina (43 percent to 19 percent), Wisconsin (27 percent to 26 percent), and Colorado (20 percent to 19 percent). The numbers show a stark contrast in the character of participation as petitioners and respondents. Where individuals dominated the ranks of petitioners, the same cannot be said of respondents. While still constituting the largest percentage of actors, government and businesses do participate at higher levels as respondents than as petitioners.

It is interesting to note that interest groups are virtually non-existent as petitioners and respondents. In no state do interest groups constitute any more than 1 percent of petitioners or respondents. Apparently, interest groups do not view participation as direct litigants to be an effective strategy to pursue their goals in state supreme courts. Groups use other methods to achieve their policy and maintenance goals, including lobbying of the state legislature and grass-roots mobilization efforts. Groups may believe that, if they are going to allocate valuable resources to litigation, they may achieve greater impact by pursuing cases through the federal courts, or through participation as *amicus*. I do not suggest that this is a complete explanation for the lack of group participation as litigants. There are a myriad of factors that may explain these data, but a primary reason may be cost. Litigation is expensive, and participation as *amicus* is a more economical way to allocate resources. This becomes even more clear when I turn to the descriptive data in the following section and discuss what actors participate as *amici curiae*. However, before addressing *amici curiae*, I discuss the substantive focus of those participating as litigants.

While I have identified, in broad terms, who the litigants are, the question of their actual interest remains. In most states, the largest category of litigants are business interests followed closely by governmental interests. Looking at petitioner interests, outlined in Table 4.5, the two largest categories are business and government. In six of the seven states, actors that focus on business or economic activity are the largest category. The most significant exception is Colorado, where governmental interests outnumber business interests. The only other interest category that could be identified in sizeable numbers were interests focusing on health and medical concerns, and even that category is quite small. The largest category, as a percentage of all interests, is unidentified. The unidentified interests are overwhelmingly individual litigants, whose interest could not be determined because they do not have any group or corporate affiliation.

Table 4.6 provides a strikingly similar picture for respondents. Again, Colorado is the only state in which government interests outnumber business interests. However, unlike petitioner interests, business and government interests participate in equal numbers in Michigan as respondents. Other respondent interests are not well represented save for Health and Medical interests, which have a non-trivial presence in Kansas, Michigan, Wisconsin, and New Jersey.

**Table 4.5**
**Interest Classification, Petitioner**

| | State | | | | | | |
|---|---|---|---|---|---|---|---|
| | *Alabama* | *Colorado* | *Kansas* | *Michigan* | *Wisconsin* | *New Jersey* | *South Carolina* |
| Business/Commercial | 23 | 32 | 36 | 35 | 33 | 38 | 26 |
| Government | 13 | 36 | 20 | 18 | 20 | 22 | 24 |
| Health/Medical | 4 | 2 | 1 | 2 | 0 | 2 | 0 |
| Labor | 1 | 1 | 1 | 1 | 4 | 2 | 0 |
| Civil Rights/Liberties | 1 | 0 | 0 | 0 | 0 | 0 | 0 |
| Public Affairs/Good Govt. | 1 | 0 | 0 | 0 | 1 | 1 | 6 |
| Religious | 0 | 0 | 1 | 2 | 0 | 0 | 0 |
| Legal | 0 | 0 | 0 | 1 | 0 | 0 | 0 |
| Other | 1 | 3 | 0 | 1 | 7 | 5 | 2 |
| Unidentified | 124 | 72 | 93 | 44 | 69 | 78 | 74 |

**Table 4.6**
**Interest Classification, Respondent**

| | State | | | | | | |
|---|---|---|---|---|---|---|---|
| | *Alabama* | *Colorado* | *Kansas* | *Michigan* | *Wisconsin* | *New Jersey* | *South Carolina* |
| Business/Commercial | 49 | 52 | 47 | 25 | 41 | 43 | 36 |
| Government | 26 | 57 | 38 | 25 | 38 | 28 | 26 |
| Health/Medical | 5 | 1 | 17 | 7 | 10 | 8 | 2 |
| Labor | 0 | 0 | 0 | 0 | 2 | 2 | 0 |
| Civil Rights/Liberties | 1 | 0 | 0 | 0 | 0 | 0 | 0 |
| Public Affairs/Good Govt. | 0 | 0 | 0 | 0 | 0 | 1 | 2 |
| Religious | 0 | 1 | 0 | 0 | 1 | 0 | 0 |
| Legal | 1 | 1 | 0 | 2 | 2 | 3 | 0 |
| Other | 0 | 0 | 0 | 2 | 1 | 1 | 1 |
| Unidentified | 68 | 155 | 65 | 58 | 67 | 37 | 29 |

Overall, the picture that emerges of the interests of the actors participating as petitioners and respondents is that they are nearly identical. The dominant interests are those that focus on commercial and governmental issues, and to a lesser extent medical and health concerns. Despite the participation by these actors, most of those participating as both petitioners and respondents are individuals. Groups are notably absent from direct litigation, choosing instead to participate more often as *amici curiae*. With a sense of those participating as litigants, in the next section I turn to the identity of those participating as *amici curiae*.

### *Amici Curiae*

The number of cases, briefs, and *amici* across all states are depicted in Figure 4.1. There were a total of 7,404 distinct arguments made in 994 *amicus* briefs filed in 644 cases decided on the merits.

Further, I classified those participating as *amicus* into distinct categories. As Table 4.7 shows quite clearly, the largest category of participants in all states, as expected, is interest groups. The second largest category in two states, Michigan and South Carolina, is business interests, while in the five other states, state level governmental entities are the second largest participants as *amici*, save for Colorado where business interests and state government participated with equal frequency. It is not surprising to find these actors represented in these proportions, but it is interesting to note the sizable representation of both business interests and governmental entities as *amici* and as litigants. Of course, I expected to see businesses as respondents in large proportions, serving as the subject of consumer suits and liability claims, but they are also present as petitioners in substantial numbers. More interesting is the participation by businesses as *amici*. Clearly, business interests view the courts as an important forum for pursuing their claims. Individuals made up the smallest proportion of those participating as *amici*, across all states.

Having identified the actors participating through the filing of *amicus* briefs, I turn to the specific interests of those third parties. As Table 4.8 shows, the *amici* come from a broad range of issue areas. The two most prevalent interests are those *amici* representing business and governmental interests. Somewhat surprisingly, labor was a rather infrequent actor, even in Michigan, where labor interests have a long history, and where one might expect more active participation in the courts. Their sparse participation may reflect a desire to allocate resources to lobbying the state legislature or involvement in other forums in which they may be more successful. Another interesting finding is the high degree of participation by legal interests, including state bars and other associations representing sectors of the legal community, such as criminal defense and prosecuting attorneys.

**Figure 4.1**
*Amicus Curiae* **Participation in Seven State Supreme Courts (Selected Cases), 1986–1995**

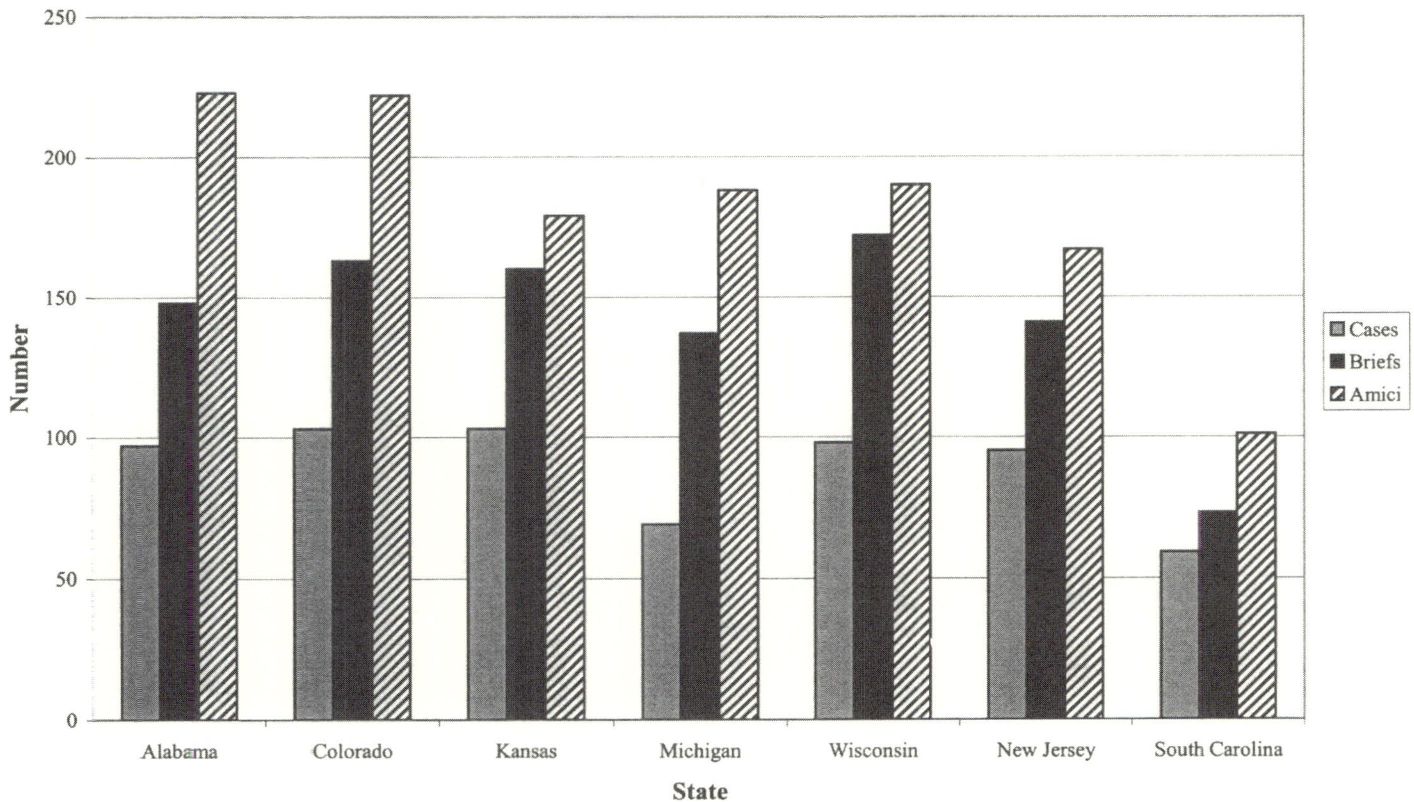

Table 4.7
Actor Classification, *Amici Curiae*

| | State | | | | | | |
|---|---|---|---|---|---|---|---|
| | *Alabama* | *Colorado* | *Kansas* | *Michigan* | *Wisconsin* | *New Jersey* | *South Carolina* |
| Business/Corporation | 42 | 25 | 12 | 39 | 9 | 14 | 17 |
| Government | | | | | | | |
| State | 50 | 25 | 18 | 10 | 17 | 32 | 11 |
| City | 10 | 21 | 2 | 0 | 1 | 2 | 1 |
| Municipality | 2 | 24 | 4 | 0 | 2 | 15 | 2 |
| Other | 3 | 1 | 1 | 3 | 0 | 6 | 3 |
| Group | 98 | 120 | 135 | 125 | 163 | 110 | 63 |
| Individual | 10 | 7 | 7 | 9 | 1 | 5 | 1 |
| Other | 2 | 0 | 1 | 0 | 1 | 5 | 0 |
| **Total Parties** | 221 | 223 | 180 | 189 | 187 | 189 | 102 |
| **Total *Amicus* Briefs** | 147 | 158 | 160 | 139 | 161 | 160 | 74 |
| **Total Cases** | 97 | 103 | 103 | 67 | 98 | 96 | 61 |
| **Mean Briefs/Case** | 1.52 | 1.53 | 1.55 | 2.01 | 1.87 | 1.76 | 1.28 |
| **Mean Parties/Brief** | 1.5 | 1.41 | 1.13 | 1.34 | 1.20 | 1.18 | 1.32 |
| **Mean Parties/Case** | 2.28 | 2.19 | 1.75 | 2.70 | 2.26 | 2.36 | 1.69 |

Table 4.8
Interest Classification, *Amici Curiae*

| | State | | | | | | |
|---|---|---|---|---|---|---|---|
| | *Alabama* | *Colorado* | *Kansas* | *Michigan* | *Wisconsin* | *New Jersey* | *South Carolina* |
| Business/Commercial | 73 | 34 | 49 | 69 | 40 | 37 | 37 |
| Government | 80 | 83 | 36 | 28 | 44 | 41 | 29 |
| Health/Medical | 8 | 8 | 14 | 5 | 16 | 10 | 5 |
| Labor | 3 | 5 | 4 | 8 | 6 | 9 | 0 |
| Civil Rights/Liberties | 2 | 17 | 14 | 17 | 19 | 23 | 1 |
| Public Affairs/Good Govt. | 5 | 6 | 2 | 2 | 14 | 5 | 0 |
| Religious | 0 | 0 | 0 | 1 | 0 | 0 | 0 |
| Legal | 30 | 56 | 45 | 34 | 36 | 49 | 15 |
| Women | 10 | 5 | 1 | 3 | 2 | 2 | 5 |
| Other | 1 | 1 | 3 | 11 | 6 | 7 | 5 |
| Unidentified | 9 | 8 | 9 | 11 | 4 | 6 | 5 |

Other interests were represented as well, though not at levels that I expected. Groups interested in the protection of civil liberties did file a number of briefs in five of the seven states, and it is interesting that the two states in which there was almost no presence by such groups were the two Southern states: Alabama and South Carolina. It is precisely these groups that sought to redress their grievances through the courts in the South beginning in the 1930s and 1940s. Those efforts were largely targeted at the federal courts, and the low level of participation in state supreme courts during the late 1980s and early 1990s may be because these groups have reached a point where they can more effectively pursue policy through state legislatures, or because they still find state courts an inhospitable environment and continue to use the federal courts. In the following section, having discussed some of the broad patterns of participation by *amici*, I turn to the hypotheses regarding arguments offered by litigants and *amici*.

## RESULTS AND DISCUSSION

Throughout this work, I have argued that groups participating as *amici* behave strategically, making arguments that will help further their goals. This assumption does not so clearly apply to litigants, who are not necessarily able, nor do they desire, to pursue broader policy goals that *amici* follow. Litigants' primary goal is to win the case. As a result, they argue all points that they believe will help them win. That will usually include arguments from one or more legal categories—reference to precedent, state or federal constitutions, statutes, and threshold issues. But litigants may also determine that it is to their advantage to include information about policy consequences, the preferences of the public, or the possible actions of other institutions, both state and federal. In this chapter, I address the arguments made in litigant briefs, comparing them to the arguments made in *amicus* briefs. I restate the hypotheses first outlined in Chapter 3, drawing conclusions about the behavior of both litigants and *amici curiae*. Table 4.9 lists the hypotheses that are tested later in this chapter.

*Hypothesis 1* and *Hypothesis 2* center on the behavior of all actors. *Hypothesis 1* holds that: *Litigant and* amicus *briefs will contain more arguments about state statutes and constitutions than federal statutes and the U.S. Constitution.* State supreme courts deal primarily with issues of state law and, as a result, the arguments contained in the briefs of litigants and *amici* should contain more references to issues related to state statutes and the state constitution than federal statutes and the U.S. Constitution. It is this information that will be of most use to justices in deciding the case at hand and will therefore be the most frequent legal arguments made by all actors.

The data on litigants and *amici*, shown in Table 4.10, largely support *Hypothesis 1*. Across all states, litigants overwhelmingly devote a greater

Table 4.9
Overview of Chapter Four Hypotheses

| | |
|---|---|
| **Hypothesis 1** | Litigant and *amicus* briefs will contain more arguments about state statutes and constitutions than federal statutes and the United States Constitution. |
| **Hypothesis 2** | Litigant and *amicus* briefs will contain more arguments about state institutions than federal institutions. |
| **Hypothesis 3** | *Amici curiae* will provide proportionately more arguments per brief about the policy consequences of the court's decisions. |
| **Hypothesis 3a** | *Amici curiae* will provide proportionately more arguments per brief about the preferences of other state institutional actors than litigants. |
| **Hypothesis 4** | Litigant briefs will contain more arguments than *amicus* briefs. |
| **Hypothesis 5** | When groups participate as litigants and *amici curiae* in states with the ballot initiative, cases will contain more arguments about policy than cases in states without the initiative. However, *amici* are expected to behave more strategically than litigants. As a result, *amici* will provide more policy arguments in their briefs than litigants in states that have the ballot initiative. |
| **Hypothesis 6** | When groups participate as litigants and *amici* in states without the ballot initiative cases will contain more arguments about institutional actors than cases filed in states that allow the initiative. Again, *amici* will provide more institutional arguments in their briefs than litigants in states without the initiative. |
| **Hypothesis 7** | In states where state supreme court justices are more accountable to the electorate, cases will contain more policy arguments than in states where they are less accountable to the electorate. This will be the case for petitioners, respondents and *amici*. |
| **Hypothesis 8** | When interest groups participate as petitioners and respondents, cases should contain more policy arguments than when other actors participate. |
| **Hypothesis 9** | When interest groups participate as *amici*, cases should contain more policy arguments than when other actors participate. |
| **Hypothesis 10** | In states where state supreme court justices are more accountable to other institutions, cases will contain more arguments about the preferences and possible actions of those institutions than in states where state supreme court justices are more accountable to the electorate. This will be the case for petitioners, respondents and *amici*. |
| **Hypothesis 11** | When interest groups participate as petitioners and respondents, cases should contain more institutional arguments than when other actors participate. |
| **Hypothesis 12** | When interest groups participate as *amici*, cases should contain more institutional arguments than when other actors participate. |

proportion of their arguments to issues involving state law than federal law. Comparing the mean number of arguments about state and federal statutory issues provides a stark contrast in the emphasis of litigants in their briefs. Looking at petitioners, the emphasis in briefs is heavily in favor of state laws by more than a factor of ten in five of the seven states. In the other states the focus is still overwhelmingly on state law. The state with the highest mean number of arguments is Kansas at 1.81 arguments per brief while the lowest is New Jersey at 0.7. The federal statute arguments range from a high in Kansas at 0.23 down to 0.04 in New Jersey. It is somewhat surprising how different New Jersey briefs appear to be than the other states, with the next lowest number of arguments coming from Michigan at 1.13 arguments per brief.

The picture is quite similar for respondents, again with the mean number of arguments centering on state statutes substantially higher than arguments about federal law. Again, Kansas has the highest mean number of state law arguments at 1.68 per brief and New Jersey the least at 0.04. This is quite similar to the results from the data collected on petitioners. As expected, state courts, though they often hear cases that involve issues of federal law, are concerned primarily with adjudicating issues of state law. As a result, we should expect the actors participating before those courts will focus on state law in their briefs. I cannot say that I expected the differences to be as stark as they appear to be, but the data do support the hypothesized behavior of litigants.

The constitutional arguments made by the litigants provides a slightly different picture, though the expectations outlined in *Hypothesis 1* are still largely supported by the data. In all but one state (Michigan) both petitioners and respondents make more arguments about state constitutions than the U.S. Constitution. For petitioners, the arguments range from a high of 0.73 in New Jersey to a low of 0.45 in Alabama. For respondents, the state with the highest mean number of state constitutional arguments is again New Jersey (0.84) and the lowest is South Carolina (0.46). The mean number of arguments from petitioners focusing on the U.S. Constitution range from a high in Kansas of 0.46 briefs per case to a low of 0.33 in South Carolina. The range for respondents runs from a high of 0.46 in both Colorado and Kansas to a low of 0.17 in New Jersey. While the data support the hypothesis, it is curious that Kansas tends to rank near or at the top for most categories and New Jersey is near the bottom in most categories.

The data from Michigan are also intriguing. The means are identical, at 0.39 constitutional arguments per brief (state and U.S.) by petitioners and 0.37 arguments per brief by respondents. I am at a loss as to why Michigan differs from the other states, and how it is that they would have identical means. However, the results from the rest of the states support *Hypothesis 3.1* that litigants will make more arguments about state law and state constitutions than federal statutes and the U.S. Constitution.

Table 4.10
Mean Constitutional and Statutory Arguments by Petitioners, Respondents, and *Amici Curiae*, 1986–1995

| | State | | | | | | |
|---|---|---|---|---|---|---|---|
| | *Alabama* | *Colorado* | *Kansas* | *Michigan* | *Wisconsin* | *New Jersey* | *South Carolina* |
| **State Statutes** | | | | | | | |
| *Petitioner* | 1.59 | 1.35 | 1.81 | 1.13 | 1.33 | 0.7 | 1.46 |
| *Respondent* | 1.53 | 1.17 | 1.68 | 1.22 | 1.32 | 0.55 | 1.59 |
| Amicus Curiae | 1.46 | 1.18 | 1.18 | 0.98 | 1.02 | 0.83 | 0.97 |
| **Federal Statutes** | | | | | | | |
| *Petitioner* | 0.1 | 0.13 | 0.23 | 0.07 | 0.04 | 0.13 | 0.11 |
| *Respondent* | 0.11 | 0.16 | 0.17 | 0.07 | 0.09 | 0.04 | 0.07 |
| Amicus Curiae | 0.14 | 0.12 | 0.15 | 0.15 | 0.11 | 0.19 | 0.14 |
| **State Constitution** | | | | | | | |
| *Petitioner* | 0.45 | 0.61 | 0.54 | 0.39 | 0.43 | 0.73 | 0.62 |
| *Respondent* | 0.52 | 0.53 | 0.47 | 0.37 | 0.50 | 0.84 | 0.46 |
| Amicus Curiae | 0.15 | 0.51 | 0.41 | 0.35 | 0.35 | 0.49 | 0.47 |
| **Federal Constitution** | | | | | | | |
| *Petitioner* | 0.34 | 0.43 | 0.49 | 0.39 | 0.35 | 0.46 | 0.33 |
| *Respondent* | 0.28 | 0.46 | 0.46 | 0.37 | 0.33 | 0.17 | 0.39 |
| Amicus Curiae | 0.67 | 0.38 | 0.39 | 0.32 | 0.18 | 0.44 | 0.3 |

The picture that emerges when looking at the legal emphasis of *amici curiae* is slightly different. The mean number of state statutory arguments per brief ranges from 0.83 in New Jersey to 1.46 in Alabama. This is significantly higher in each state than arguments about federal statutes, which range from 0.11 per brief in Wisconsin to 0.19 in New Jersey. The differences are rather striking. The range of the mean number of state statutory arguments is quite large when compared to the federal statutory arguments. Also, it is interesting that the mean number of arguments about state law is lowest in New Jersey, but the mean number of arguments involving federal statutes is highest in that state. I suspect this is likely the result of the nature of the sample of cases drawn from the state, and I am not eager to draw any substantive inferences from these data. The differences between the states are not that large, but it is at least worth noting the disparity.

Most issues that are adjudicated in state supreme courts will involve issues of state law, and it is to be expected that litigants and *amici* refer to that law in their briefs. Petitioners and respondents devote generally the same amount of space, in total, to those issues across states. This pattern is also exhibited in *amicus* briefs, mirroring litigants quite closely. This may not be so surprising to the reader, but it suggests that *amici* apparently feel that they must make a substantial effort to include legal argument in their briefs. Those briefs that focus solely on policy arguments, to the exclusion of other arguments, may not be taken as seriously by judges. Including legal arguments, showing justices that they are competent, sophisticated, and professional, may serve to increase the likelihood that the policy arguments will be taken more seriously by the court than if the *amicus* had included *only* policy arguments.

Similarly, when referencing the potential actions of other actors, litigants and *amici* are both more likely to discuss state actors. It is reasonable to assume that state supreme court justices will be more concerned with how the governor and state legislature might react to decisions of the court than federal institutions. They will likely be better informed about the cases confronting the high court in that state and possess the ability to affect the policy handed down by the court more quickly than federal institutions such as the Supreme Court. Other state level institutions, such as the legislature and governor, are also better able to monitor whether or not the state supreme court is interpreting state law consistently.

This is not to suggest that state supreme court justices do not care how the Supreme Court may react to their decisions; it is expected that they do. However, only a small percentage of cases appealed from state supreme courts every year are granted review by the Supreme Court. Not only has it traditionally been highly unlikely that any single decision of a state supreme court will be reviewed by the Supreme Court, that possibility is becoming even more remote in recent years as the Court has made a clear, and voluntary, effort to decrease the number of cases that it accepts for review. It is more likely that the state legislature and governor will respond to the decisions of their respective state high court, ultimately affecting the efficacy of the policy handed down by the court. Consequently, *Hypothesis 2* holds that: *Litigant and* amicus *briefs will contain more arguments about state institutions than federal institutions.*

Table 4.11 displays the data on the mean number of arguments involving state and federal institutions. The data suggest a somewhat mixed picture of the emphasis placed on institutional arguments. In four (Alabama, Colorado, Wisconsin, and South Carolina) of the seven states, the mean number of arguments that address the preferences and potential responses of other branches of state government are substantially higher than those arguments about the possible actions of federal institutions. The data from Michigan, a merit selection state, show that the litigants make more arguments about state institutions than federal institutions, but *amici* in that state average half as many arguments about state institutions than federal institutions. Moreover, the litigants make more state institutional arguments than *amici* by a large margin, with petitioners averaging 0.45, respondents 0.3, and *amici* only 0.18 arguments per brief.

The behavior of petitioners, respondents, and *amici* does not comport with the hypothesized behavior in two states: Kansas and New Jersey. In New Jersey, the mean number of state institutional arguments is less than the federal arguments made by petitioners and *amici,* and only respondents make more state arguments than federal. In Kansas, the difference is even more conspicuous, as the average number of federal arguments is equal to the average state arguments for respondents (0.47 state and federal), and greater for petitioners (0.35 state and 0.49 federal) and *amici* (0.35 state and 0.41 federal). I can offer little in the way of explanation as to why this is the case in Kansas. However, it does follow the activity of *amici,* who also provided proportionately greater attention to federal institutions than to state institutions. This may be due to a relatively weak state legislature and governor, or perhaps it may just be that there is little history of conflict between the branches in the state. In such a case, there would be little purpose in attempting to sway the court with references to the possibility that the decision might be overturned. I point this out because in *Hypothesis 3A* I outlined my expectation that *amici curiae* will make more state institutional arguments than litigants. I deal with this at greater length later in this chapter, but it is worth noting that, at least for Kansas, the hypothesis is not supported by these data.

Where *Hypotheses 1* and *2* address the differences in the types of information that *all* actors—petitioners, respondents and *amici*—are expected to include in their briefs, the remaining hypotheses focus on the expected differences *between* litigants and *amici curiae*. *Hypothesis 3* states: Amici Curiae *will provide more arguments about the policy consequences of the court's*

Table 4.11
Mean State and Federal Institution Arguments by Petitioners, Respondents, and *Amici Curiae*, 1986–1995

| | **State** | | | | | | |
|---|---|---|---|---|---|---|---|
| | *Alabama* | *Colorado* | *Kansas* | *Michigan* | *Wisconsin* | *New Jersey* | *South Carolina* |
| **State Institutions** | | | | | | | |
| *Petitioner* | 0.39 | 0.46 | 0.35 | 0.45 | 0.39 | 0.33 | 0.32 |
| *Respondent* | 0.45 | 0.5 | 0.47 | 0.3 | 0.49 | 0.46 | 0.44 |
| Amicus Curiae | 0.54 | 0.58 | 0.35 | 0.18 | 0.32 | 0.36 | 1.01 |
| **Federal Institutions** | | | | | | | |
| *Petitioner* | 0.07 | 0.2 | 0.49 | 0.13 | 0.17 | 0.63 | 0.05 |
| *Respondent* | 0.1 | 0.23 | 0.47 | 0.12 | 0.13 | 0.42 | 0.11 |
| Amicus Curiae | 0.16 | 0.29 | 0.41 | 0.35 | 0.22 | 0.46 | 0.12 |

*decisions than litigants*. One of the stated purposes for the participation of *amici curiae* is to notify the court of issues that may not be included in the briefs of litigants. This has often meant informing courts of the larger social and political implications of the case before them and the potential impact of their decisions. As I have shown here, the vast majority of those actors participating as *amici* are interest groups. Interest groups and professional associations often represent large, or particularly powerful, segments of the population, and have the resources and inclination to provide exactly this information.

The same justification for *Hypothesis 3* supports the reasoning behind *Hypothesis 3A*, which holds that: Amici curiae *will provide more arguments per brief about the preferences and possible responses to the court's decisions of other state institutions*. Again, *amici* are provided with the incentive to provide this type of information where the litigants are not so motivated, or not entirely free to make these arguments. This is not to say that litigants do not make such arguments, but they are not necessarily encouraged to do so. *Amici* are expected to provide this information. As the data show, the vast majority of those participating as *amici curiae* are interest groups. Groups have the resources to conduct the research and to become involved in the direction of policy, whereas other actors are more likely to be more narrowly focused and do not have the resources to participate in this manner.

The results are reported in Table 4.12. Addressing the policy arguments made by the actors first, the data provide qualified support for *Hypothesis 3*. In four (Alabama, Colorado, New Jersey, and South Carolina) of the seven states, *amici* provide more arguments than either petitioners or respondents. Though the results are mixed, and not entirely supportive of the hypothesis, the pattern exhibited by the data is suggestive. Two of the three states where litigants include information about the policy implications of the court's decisions in their briefs at higher rates than *amici* are states where state supreme court justices are chosen in non-partisan election systems. Kansas is the third state and justices are chosen via merit selection. The hypothesis is supported by the data from the two states where justices are chosen directly by the other branches of state government (governor and state legislature), by the one non-partisan election state (Alabama), and the other merit election state (Colorado). It is slightly curious why *amici* in one merit election state make more arguments, on average, than litigants, but in the other merit state they do not. However, it is telling that in gubernatorial appointment and legislative election state, *amici* average more policy arguments than litigants.

It is possible that in New Jersey and South Carolina, *amici* view the presentation of information about the policy consequences of a decision as strategically as information about the preferences of those other actors (governor and legislature). By providing this information, although

Table 4.12

**Mean Policy and Institutional Arguments by Petitioners, Respondents, and *Amici Curiae*, 1986–1995**

| | State | | | | | | |
|---|---|---|---|---|---|---|---|
| | *Alabama* | *Colorado* | *Kansas* | *Michigan* | *Wisconsin* | *New Jersey* | *South Carolina* |
| **Policy** | | | | | | | |
| *Petitioner* | 0.43 | 0.83 | 1.27 | 1.19 | 1.31 | 0.59 | 0.47 |
| *Respondent* | 0.44 | 0.63 | 1.31 | 1.13 | 1.31 | 0.4 | 0.44 |
| Amicus Curiae | 0.67 | 0.92 | 1.16 | 1.06 | 1.20 | 0.9 | 0.78 |
| **Institutions** | | | | | | | |
| *Petitioner* | 0.39 | 0.46 | 0.35 | 0.45 | 0.39 | 0.33 | 0.32 |
| *Respondent* | 0.45 | 0.5 | 0.47 | 0.30 | 0.49 | 0.46 | 0.44 |
| Amicus Curiae | 0.54 | 0.58 | 0.35 | 0.18 | 0.32 | 0.36 | 1.01 |
| **Total Arguments** | | | | | | | |
| *Petitioner* | 7.69 | 8.06 | 11.55 | 7.66 | 8.45 | 8.25 | 7.66 |
| *Respondent* | 8.32 | 7.89 | 11.39 | 8.09 | 8.77 | 8.51 | 7.85 |
| Amicus Curiae | 6.72 | 7.77 | 7.43 | 7.75 | 6.28 | 6.82 | 7.74 |

couched as policy arguments, it may serve the interests of *amici* by alerting the court to the consequences of the case, and implicitly, how those other actors would respond to the court's decision. So, it is possible that in those states that *amici* (and litigants) are making arguments in such a way that they do not explicitly reference the governor or legislature, but provide some discussion of potential policy outcomes that the court is aware is of serious interest to those actors.

The previous discussion suggests that *amici* are expected to provide information that is not contained in litigant briefs, thereby supplementing the record for the justices. *Amici* have a defined and potentially narrow role. They are able to make decisions about the information to give the court, something that would not necessarily enter into the decision making of the litigants who will make any and all arguments that will further their cause. As a result, briefs filed by *amici* will be more focused, making fewer arguments than briefs filed by litigants. *Hypothesis 4* states that: *Litigant briefs will contain more distinct arguments than* amicus *briefs, across all states.*

In addition to the number of policy and institutional arguments made by litigants and *amici,* Table 4.12 shows the mean number of total arguments for petitioners, respondents, and *amici curiae.* Looking at the mean arguments of each actor by state, the data offer substantial support for *Hypothesis 3.4.* Across all states, save for petitioners in South Carolina and Michigan, petitioners and respondents make more arguments, on average, than do *amici*—in most cases by a large margin. In South Carolina, all parties make approximately the same number of arguments, with *amici* placing in between petitioners and respondents. The difference is quite small, with the range between the three actors in that state less than 0.2 arguments per brief.

The data from Michigan present a similar picture. Here also, the mean number of arguments made by *amici* fall in between those of petitioners and respondents. The difference in average arguments by these actors is rather small as well with petitioners at 7.66 arguments per brief, *amici* at 7.75, and respondents at 8.09. The difference between the actors in Michigan is only slightly more than that in South Carolina, at just over 0.4 arguments per brief.

In the other five states, litigants make, on average, more arguments than do *amici,* and by a large margin in four of the five. The difference in the number of arguments is striking in Alabama, Kansas, Wisconsin, and New Jersey. *Amici* average almost a full argument less per brief in Alabama than the petitioners, who average almost eight arguments. By far the greatest disparity in arguments is in Kansas where litigants average approximately four arguments per brief more than *amici.* The difference in mean arguments in both New Jersey and Wisconsin fall between Kansas and Alabama. It is worth recognizing that though petitioners and respondents average more arguments than *amici* in Colorado, the gap between the actors is quite small—less than 0.3 arguments per brief.

While not explicitly hypothesized, a pattern among the data appears. In five of the seven states, respondents average more arguments per brief than petitioners. In only Colorado and Kansas, both merit selection states, do petitioners make more arguments than respondents. I can offer no explanation as to why the selection system should influence the number of arguments made by litigants and *amici*, and specifically why the merit states should be different than states where other systems are used. Also, the differences here are rather small, with petitioners and respondents within 0.2 arguments per brief. While there are differences, they are small and may not be the result of institutional differences, so they should be interpreted with some caution.

The data presented to assess *Hypotheses 1* through *4* are largely supported by the data. However, there are issues raised by these data that deserve more attention. One aspect of the data that I think deserves discussion is the pattern that emerges from Kansas, Michigan, and Wisconsin. The information from litigants and *amici* appear to be quite similar. *Hypotheses 3, 3A,* and *4* do not predict these states correctly. What is most striking is that, looking at the policy and institutional arguments made by actors in those states, the petitioners and respondents make more arguments of each type than *amici curiae*. In both Michigan and Wisconsin, justices are selected on non-partisan ballots. In Kansas, justices are selected by the merit selection system. While the data from Colorado do offer support for the hypotheses, the results are not particularly compelling. For policy and institutional arguments, the means across actors are quite similar.

Petitioners, respondents, and *amici* behave similarly in non-partisan and merit selection states. This suggests that those participating in those states may view judicial accountability similarly. If these actors are making arguments at similar levels, then it can be extrapolated that *amici* do not feel that providing information about the policy consequences or preferences of other elite actors will be of use to justices, or particularly influential when coming from *amici curiae*.

This is not a trivial result. Throughout, I have made the argument that *amici* exist to provide information that justices might not otherwise get from litigants. With these data I am not able to say anything about the substantive message being conveyed by *amici*, but I can draw conclusions about the format and structure of their briefs. The inference is that selection system may operate to influence legal actors in those states where they are presumably less directly accountable electorally to a particular constituency. Whether it is the governor, legislature, or the public, *amici* provide fewer arguments about the potential implications of their decisions. Where litigants and *amici* perceive there to be a more proximate and direct connection to the electorate (partisan election system—Alabama) or to other institutions (governor—New Jersey; legislature—South Carolina), then they appear to behave more as hypothesized.

## Modeling the Behavior of Litigants and *Amici Curiae*

*Hypotheses 1* through *4* focus on the behavior of the different actors participating before the courts. In evaluating these hypotheses, the results were mixed. The primary focus of this chapter so far has been on the general differences between those that are direct parties to a suit and those actors that file *amicus curiae* briefs. I have provided a broad outline of differences between petitioners, respondents, and *amici*. However, this discussion can be taken a step farther, focusing on how individuals, groups, businesses, and government actors, participating as litigants and *amici*, behave in different institutional settings. With the remaining hypotheses I explore the behavior of these actors.

In this section, I restate those hypotheses from Chapter 3 that motivate the model I develop in this chapter. *Hypothesis 5* states: *When groups participate as litigants and* amici curiae *in states with the ballot initiative, cases will contain more arguments about policy than cases in states without the initiative. However, because of the traditional role that* amici *serve, they will make more policy arguments than litigants.* Where a state uses the ballot initiative, providing for at least the possibility of a public override of decisions of the state supreme court, litigants and *amici* will make arguments to the court that alert them to the potential policy consequences of their decision. I have already discussed the theoretical foundation for expecting groups to provide different information in their briefs before the court, particularly as *amici curiae*. In short, groups have both the resources and inclination to behave strategically, serving as a source of information to the court that it might not otherwise obtain from other sources. Where the public has a direct role in policy making, as they do in states with the ballot initiative, I expect justices to be more concerned about policy outcomes and the impact on the public. Consequently, groups will be more likely to behave in sophisticated, strategic ways than other actors, making arguments that will be useful, and potentially influential.

In contrast, in states that do not use the initiative, litigants and *amici* will be less likely to make arguments about specific policy outcomes. In these states, groups will be more likely to make arguments that inform justices of the potential actions of other institutional actors. Justices will be less concerned about the possibility of their decisions being overturned by the public through a popular initiative. *Hypothesis 6* holds: *When groups participate as litigants and* amici *in states without the ballot initiative, cases will contain more institutional arguments than in states do use the initiative.* Amici *will make more of these arguments than litigants.*

*Hypotheses 5* and *6* center on the role of the ballot initiative in ordering the behavior of legal actors. The remaining hypotheses address the role of judicial selection mechanisms and how the identity of the actors participating before the courts influences how they construct their briefs. *Hypothesis 7* states that: *In states where justices are more accountable to the electorate, cases will contain more policy arguments than in states where they are less accountable to the electorate. This will hold for petitioners, respondents, and* amici. The argument is straightforward. Justices will be most concerned about the potential responses by the public to the decisions of the court through the ballot box.

*Hypotheses 8* and *9* flow from *Hypothesis 7. Hypothesis 8* holds that: *When interest groups participate as petitioners and respondents, cases should contain more policy arguments than when other actors participate. Hypothesis 9* is: *When interest groups participate as* amici, *cases should contain more policy arguments than when other actors participate as* amici. These two hypotheses, taken together, address the differences between groups and all other actors. Groups are more strategic than other actors and offer information that they believe will be important to justices in reaching decisions. I submit that, regardless of whether they are petitioners, respondents, or *amici*, groups will be more likely to make policy and institutional arguments than businesses, government, or individuals. Other actors do not have the financial and legal resources that groups do, but more importantly, they do not have the incentive to use the courts in the same way as groups. Therefore, we should see more strategic, sophisticated behavior from those groups.

*Hypotheses 10, 11,* and *12* mirror *7, 8,* and *9,* except that these three focus on the institutional arguments made by litigants and *amici*. Again, groups will behave more strategically than other actors and make more arguments about the positions, and possible responses, of the governor and state legislature, in those states where justices are elected or appointed directly by the governor or legislature. In the following section, I discuss how I operationalize the models and the details of the variables included in these models.

In order to evaluate these hypotheses, I make use of a Negative Binomial Regression Model.[14] I estimate six different models, one for each of the dependent variables: The number of arguments about state institutional actors made by petitioners, respondents, and *amici curiae*; and the number of policy arguments by petitioners, respondents, and *amici curiae*. The independent variables included in the model are of two general categories: actor variables and institutional variables. These variables are listed in Table 4.13. The actor variables are the number of individuals, the number of businesses or corporations, the number of governmental actors (either state, city, county, or municipality), the number of local interest groups, and the number of national interest groups filing briefs. The institutional variables focus on the role of the public in determining policy and the various selection mechanisms used by the states in selecting and retaining state supreme court justices. There is a dichotomous variable for the ballot initiative, coded as 1 if the state has the initiative, and 0 otherwise. There are also several variables to capture the effect of the selection system on the behavior of actors participating before the courts. These are dichotomous variables for each of the five selection methods, coded as 1 if the state uses that method to chooses its state supreme court justices, and 0 otherwise. With these models, I am able to assess the behavior of each of the various actors participating in each forum, making inferences about the degree of strategic behavior by the actors.

The results for the institutions model are presented in Table 4.14. Looking at the actor variables for each of the three models, clearly whether or

**Table 4.13**
**Variable Explanations for Negative Binomial Models**

| Variable | Explanation |
|---|---|
| **Dependent Variables** | |
| **Policy Arguments:** | Number of Policy Arguments in a given case made by Petitioners, Respondents, and Amici. |
| **Institutional Arguments:** | Number of Arguments about State Institutions in a given case made by Petitioners, Respondents, and Amici. |
| **Independent Variables** | |
| **Local Interest Group:** | Number of Interest Groups Participating as Amicus. |
| **National Interest Group:** | Number of Interest Groups Participating as Amicus. |
| **State/Government:** | Number of Governmental Actors Participating as Amicus. |
| **Business/Corporation:** | Number of Businesses Participating as Amicus. |
| **Partisan Election:** | Dichotomous Variable Coded as 1 if a Partisan Election State, 0 Otherwise. |
| **Non-Partisan Election:** | Dichotomous Variable Coded as 1 if a Non-Partisan Election State, 0 Otherwise. |
| **Merit Election:** | Dichotomous Variable Coded as 1 if a Merit Election State, 0 Otherwise. |
| **Gubernatorial Election:** | Dichotomous Variable Coded as 1 if a Gubernatorial Election State, 0 Otherwise. |
| **Ballot Initiative:** | Dichotomous Variable Coded as 1 if a State uses the Ballot Initiative, 0 Otherwise. |

not a local interest group participated as *amicus curiae* is highly significant and signed in the expected direction. However, the national interest group, state, and business variables do not reach statistical significance. So, as the number of local groups participating as *amici curiae* increases, the probability of additional arguments in a case increases as well. Looking at the petitioner and respondent models, the picture is not as clear. Local groups participating as respondents increases the probability of additional institutional arguments, but interest group participation as petitioners does not. It is interesting that the local groups appear to behave more strategically than national groups when participating as *amici*. One might think that national groups, with greater financial resources and with a keener eye toward national policy strategies, would behave in more strategic ways than local interest groups. However, local groups are closer to the situation than national groups, and being more intimately aware of the political environment in which they are participating, perhaps they should be expected to be more strategic than national groups precisely because they do have information and goals that differ from national groups.

What I also find interesting is the state variable for both the petitioner and respondent models. The state variable in each is signed in the expected direction and highly significant. This suggests that where the state or other governmental actors participate directly in a case, the likelihood of institutional arguments increases. Where the government is a direct participant they obviously feel compelled to include information in their briefs that alert the court to the preferences of governmental institutions, and the possible actions of those actors. This is quite interesting, as they must view their role as a direct litigant differently than they do when participating as *amici curiae*. When they file a brief as a litigant, government entities seem compelled to include arguments about how the court's decisions will affect them and what their reaction would be to the court's decision. The data do not show such a willingness when participating as *amici curiae*. Governmental interests may very well view the filing of *amicus* briefs quite differently than groups, suggesting that they have a proclivity to send important signals to the court about the repercussions of the court's decision where the state or other government actor is directly affected.

The data suggest that business actors do not behave significantly differently than individuals across all categories of participation, either as petitioners, respondents, or *amici curiae*. This is not particularly surprising. I did not expect businesses to behave strategically when participating in the courts, as they, like individuals, do not have the same incentive structure, or resources, as groups. Though they do have more financial resources than most individuals, they are unlikely to have coherent and systematic strategies for using the courts to further their ends. Therefore, they should

Table 4.14
**Parameter Estimates for Negative Binomial Models—Institutions**

| Independent Variable | Parameter Estimates for Each Model | | |
|---|---|---|---|
| | **Petitioner** | **Respondent** | ***Amicus Curiae*** |
| **Actor Variables** | | | |
| Local Interest Group | 0.309<br>(0.404) | 1.119**<br>(0.433) | 0.419**<br>(0.060) |
| National Interest Group | 0.287<br>(0.319) | 0.367<br>(0.445) | 0.322<br>(0.235) |
| State | 0.687**<br>(0.192) | 0.703**<br>(0.185) | 0.162<br>(0.198) |
| Business/Corporation | 0.122<br>(0.215) | 0.054<br>(0.214) | 0.150<br>(0.154) |
| **Institutional Variables** | | | |
| Partisan Election | 0.312<br>(0.345) | 0.122<br>(0.320) | -0.479<br>(0.263) |
| Non-Partisan Election | 0.329<br>(0.330) | -0.004<br>(0.306) | -1.224**<br>(0.263) |
| Merit | 0.443<br>(0.325) | 0.171<br>(0.302) | -0.740**<br>(0.256) |
| Gubernatorial | 0.025<br>(0.069) | 0.213<br>(0.326) | -0.892**<br>(0.273) |
| Ballot Initiative | 0.002<br>(0.205) | -0.082<br>(0.208) | 0.191<br>(0.192) |
| Constant | -1.469<br>(0.294) | -1.209<br>(0.280) | -0.376<br>(0.211) |
| $\alpha$ | 1.498** | 1.480** | 1.487** |
| Likelihood Ratio $\chi^2$ | 16.07* | 21.81** | 65.40** |

Standard Errors in Parentheses
Number of Observations: 637

*Significant at $p< .05$
**Significant at $p< .01$

not be expected to behave in ways similar to groups, structuring their briefs to capitalize on the institutional structure.

Turning to the institutional variables in the institutions models, all of the state selection mechanism variables are signed in the expected direction for the *amici* model, but virtually all of the variables for the petitioner and respondent models are signed in the opposite direction as would be expected and *none* of the variables reach statistical significance. Actors participating as petitioners or respondents apparently do not respond at all to the manner in which their state supreme court justices are selected and retained, attempting to understand their incentive structures and to play on the goals and constraints on those justices. This gets back to my previous discussion about the constraints on petitioners and respondents. They are expected to detail the main legal arguments for the justices, and this prevents them from devoting a substantial portion of their briefs to arguments about institutional actors. Thus, it is not entirely surprising that the petitioner and respondent models do not respond as well as the *amicus* model.

In the *amici* institutions model, all but the partisan election variable reach statistical significance. Essentially these variables can be interpreted to mean that the probability of having additional institutional arguments is less in these systems than in the legislative appointment system. I find that to be somewhat puzzling as I expected that selection mechanism to be significant, along with the merit and non-partisan variables. In particular the gubernatorial variable is significantly different than the legislative appointment state though I expected it to be quite similar to that system in terms of the amount of institutional arguments in cases in those states. Perhaps I should not be surprised at this finding, as I suggested that state legislatures have the added power to override decisions of state supreme courts involving state statutes by simply circumventing the decision through additional legislation. Given this additional power of state legislatures, the significance of the gubernatorial variable stands out even more.

Though the selection system variables largely support my hypotheses regarding *amicus* behavior, the effect of the ballot initiative is not as conclusive. The presence of the ballot initiative does not appear to have an effect on the probability of institutional arguments in any given case for any of the models and is signed in the opposite direction as expected in both the petitioner and *amicus* model. The ballot initiative is not often used, and state supreme court justices may not view it as a constraint on their behavior.[15] If they do not see at as a constraint, then interest groups and other, even less strategic actors, may not view it in such a light either. As a result, they will not make arguments that reflect their understanding of this institutional feature as a limitation on the behavior of state supreme court justices.

The results of the policy models are quite similar to those from the institutional models, with several notable exceptions. These results are shown in Table 4.15. Again, as in the *amicus* institutions model, the local interest group variable is highly significant, while all of the other actors are not significantly related to the number of policy arguments contained in an individual case. However, group participation as direct parties to a suit does not result in an increase in the likelihood of additional policy arguments. Interestingly, as government participation as petitioners and respondents was significantly related to the number of institutional arguments contained in a case, the number of businesses participating in a case as direct litigants is significantly related to the number of policy arguments in a case. While I did not particular expect this result from the data, it is not without a feasible explanation. While governmental actors were willing, and perhaps quite eager, to discuss their preferences, and perhaps the preferences of other institutional actors, where businesses participate as litigants, they are willing to make a higher number of policy arguments than other actors. This does not necessarily demonstrate strategic behavior, per se, on the part of business actors. On the contrary, it is quite understandable that a business would make arguments about the policy consequences of a decision of the court. Any decision of the court would possibly adversely affect the workers of a company, and possibly the economy of the state itself.

Therefore, it makes sense that businesses would make such arguments, but it is not clear why, when participating as *amici curiae,* there is not significant correlation with the arguments made by businesses and the number of policy arguments in a case. The interests of a business choosing to participate as *amici* may be quite different than groups. Businesses are not likely to participate for membership maintenance, and the arguments that they make are likely to be tailored narrowly to deal with how a case might adversely affect that business or economic sector. This is not, in and of itself, adequate explanation for why businesses do not make policy arguments when participating as *amici,* but it does suggest that where their interests are more directly affected, business interests are more willing to make those arguments that they feel will be of most use in achieving a favorable outcome on the merits. And in this case, that includes making policy arguments to supplement the legal arguments that they offer in their briefs.

The institutional variables follow a similar pattern as those shown in the institutions models. For the *amicus* policy model, in cases in non-partisan and merit states there is an increased probability of policy arguments per case than in the legislative appointment systems. However, unlike in the *amicus* institutions model, the gubernatorial variable is not significant. This is not entirely unexpected. Where *amici* viewed the state legislature as a more credible threat to the decisions of state supreme court justices, and

Table 4.15
**Parameter Estimates for Negative Binomial Regression Models—Policy**

| Independent Variable | Petitioner | Respondent | Amicus Curiae |
|---|---|---|---|
| | Parameter Estimates for Each Model | | |
| **Actor Variables** | | | |
| Local Interest Group | 0.117 | 0.383 | 0.370** |
| | (0.218) | (0.281) | (0.028) |
| National Interest Group | 0.095 | 0.274 | 0.211 |
| | (0.124) | (0.149) | (0.196) |
| State | 0.058 | 0.200 | 0.084 |
| | (0.112) | (0.115) | (0.095) |
| Business/Corporation | 0.223* | 0.329** | -0.023 |
| | (0.108) | (0.119) | (0.075) |
| **Institutional Variables** | | | |
| Partisan Election | -0.167 | -0.170 | 0.220 |
| | (0.220) | (0.229) | (0.155) |
| Non-Partisan Election | 0.788** | 0.870** | 0.395** |
| | (0.186) | (0.195) | (0.146) |
| Merit | 0.719** | 0.742** | 0.370** |
| | (0.186) | (0.195) | (0.144) |
| Gubernatorial | -0.001 | -0.157 | 0.062 |
| | (0.212) | (0.231) | (0.157) |
| Ballot Initiative | -0.297** | -0.420** | -0.028 |
| | (0.104) | (0.115) | (0.085) |
| Constant | -0.542 | -0.663 | -0.153 |
| | (0.172) | (0.187) | (0.130) |
| $\alpha$ | 0.116 | 0.259** | 0.206** |
| Likelihood Ratio $\chi^2$ | 63.32** | 75.73** | 184.26** |

Standard Errors in Parentheses
Number of Observations: 637

*Significant at $p< .05$
**Significant at $p< .01$

made more institutional arguments as a result, when it comes to policy arguments, they may not behave in ways that are distinguishable between the gubernatorial and legislative systems. It is more important to make more institutional arguments in the legislative system than in the gubernatorial system, but not so when it comes to policy arguments. The two systems elicit similar behavior from *amici* when it comes to policy arguments.

A major difference between the policy models and the institutions models is the institutional variables. In the institutions model, they were only significant for *amici*, but in the policy model the non-partisan and merit election variables are highly significant for all three categories of actors. Petitioners, respondents, and *amici* make more policy arguments in merit and non-partisan election systems. Again, the partisan variable is notable for the lack of correlation with the number of policy arguments across all three models. For all six models, the partisan election system was not significantly related to the number of policy or institutional arguments in a case. The partisan election state in this study was Alabama, and it is possible that interest groups are not as strategic there as in other states. In particular, Alabama has loose regulations governing statewide campaigns, and registration requirements for PACs and others interested in lobbying the legislature are not well organized or controlled. Thus, given the ease with which groups can lobby the legislature, it is quite plausible that groups do not participate before the courts in as sophisticated a way as they do in other systems.

Again, like the *amicus* institutions model, the ballot initiative is not significant in the *amicus* policy model. Actually, it is highly significant, but signed in the opposite direction as I expect in the petitioner and respondent policy models. As I mentioned previously, the ballot initiative should not be considered a substantial limitation on state supreme court justices, and for actors to provide fewer policy arguments in ballot initiative states there must be another explanation that is not captured by the institutional analysis performed here.

## CONCLUSION

I have included a great deal of data in this chapter on the character and behavior of litigants and *amici curiae*. I include this analysis to compare the behavior of litigants with *amici* with the intention of evaluating the possibility of strategic behavior of legal actors, with a focus on groups participating as *amici curiae*. The findings suggest that there are substantial differences in the behavior of litigants and *amici*. The conventional wisdom that *amici* become involved in cases for different reasons than litigants and make different arguments than litigants is largely borne out. *Amici* do have different motivations than litigants, and not only is status as *amicus* critical to an understanding of the behavior of legal actors, so too is the identity of those participating as *amicus*. Interest groups have different motivations from other actors that might participate as *amici curiae*. This different goal structure results in distinct patterns between *amici curiae* and the information provided. More than any other category of actor, interest groups behave strategically, making arguments that account for the institutional environment and providing information that presumably will be of greatest use to justices in achieving their policy and reelection goals. In addition to comparing the behavior of litigants and *amici*, this chapter has another goal, which is to present a more complete picture of the actors involved in these cases, providing a backdrop for the discussion of the decision making of justices.

In the next chapter, I turn my attention to these goals of state supreme court justices. The question that motivates the final chapter is: given the information provided by the various litigants and *amici*, how do justices respond to that information in deciding cases? By describing the constellation of actors involved in these state supreme courts and the arguments that they make, I will be able to better understand the resulting behavior of justices. I argued at the outset that justices are strategic seekers of policy and reelection, and the data that I have presented to this point, along with other factors to be introduced in the final chapter, allow me to evaluate this assumption.

## NOTES

1. The action taken by the Coastal Council relied primarily on the South Carolina Coastal Management Act Regulation 30–12 (a) (2), which states: "(a) The creation of commercial and residential lots strictly for private gain is not a legitimate justification for the filling of wetlands. Permit applications for the filling of wetlands and submerged lands for these purposes shall be denied, except for erosion control or boat ramps. All other dredge and fill activities not in the public interest will be discouraged."

2. *Carter v. South Carolina Coastal Council* (304 S.E. 2d 327, 1986).

3. 304 S.E. 2d 327, 1986, p. 14.

4. *Amicus* brief of National Resources Defense Council (NRDC), p. 8.

5. *Amicus* brief of National Resources Defense Council (NRDC), p. 29.

6. *Nichols v. State Farm Insurance Company* (306 S.E. 2d 616, 1986).

7. *Amicus* brief of the South Carolina Defense Trial Attorneys Association, p. 9.

8. *Amicus* brief of the South Carolina Defense Trial Attorneys Association, p. 11.

9. *Heurtebise v. Reliable Business Computers, Inc.* (549 N.W. 2d 560, 1995).

10. Brief of *Heurtebiese*, p. 6.

11. Brief of *Reliable Business Computers, Inc.*, p. 24.

12. Brief of the Association of Trial Lawyers of America, the Michigan Trial Lawyers Association, and the American Civil Liberties Union, p. 3.

13. Brief of the Association of Trial Lawyers of America, the Michigan Trial Lawyers Association, and the American Civil Liberties Union, p. 10.

14. A justification for the use of the Negative Binomial Regression is discussed in the Appendix.

15. Between 1981 and 1992 Colorado passed ten of twenty-four initiatives, and Michigan passed three of nine initiatives on the ballot in those states. Of the twenty-four states that allow for the initiative, there were only 346 initiatives voted on during this entire time period.

# CHAPTER 5

# Information and State Supreme Court Decision Making

## INTRODUCTION

In 1996, the American Bar Association formed the Commission on Separation of Powers and Judicial Independence to study politically motivated attacks on members of the judiciary. The attacks generally came from members of legislatures and interest groups and were motivated by what they perceived as judicial activism on the part of individual judges. The ABA felt that such efforts against judges had reached a point where the ability of judges to remain independent, neutral arbiters was compromised. In addition, the ABA voiced substantial concern over the rising costs associated with state judicial elections and the implications of increasing fundraising efforts on judicial independence.

These concerns are borne out by the comments of a retired California State Supreme Court Justice. In response to a question about the influence of attacks on the court and how they impact future decisions, Otto Kaus responded that "It is difficult to ignore a crocodile in your bathtub when you're shaving in the morning."[1] As this comment suggests, it is difficult, if not impossible for judges to insulate themselves from the political environment, particularly when they are continually caught between the desire to remain neutral arbitrators and the need to be reelected.

Some have suggested that state supreme court justices ought to be appointed to office and serve life tenure. As a result, they argue, justices will be immune from the criticism and attacks that often lead to the removal of those justices in retention and competitive elections. Indeed, as our legal system is currently constituted, judges are not insulated from political pressures. This fact is not lost on state supreme court judges, or the various litigants that participate before them. In fact, I argue that participants do understand that justices are sensitive to the political environment and that the arguments that they make in their briefs when participating in state supreme courts reflect their understanding of what information will be of most use to those justices, possibly leading to greater success in those courts.

In Chapter 4, I argued that interest groups are strategic actors and account for the institutional context when providing information to state supreme court justices. Similarly, I argue that state supreme court justices are strategic, behaving in ways that maximize their chances of securing favorable policy while at the same time maintaining their positions. My theory, that interest groups will provide information to justices that they believe will be of use to those justices, relies on the assumption that justices are looking for information that will assist them in their policy and reelection goals. The discussion in Chapter 4 provides qualified support that interest groups are making arguments strategically.

While the data suggest that interest groups are behaving strategically, the question of how this information is received by the justices remains. A number of important questions can be investigated. In this chapter, I focus primarily on the decision making of justices, and how cases are ultimately decided. The primary issue that motivates the discussion in this chapter is whether or not there is a greater chance of success for litigants that make certain arguments in their briefs, and whether or not *amicus* support increases the chance of success for those litigants.

In evaluating this question, I first turn to the decisions of several state supreme courts. I begin by returning to the case of *Carter v. Coastal Council* discussed at the beginning of Chapter 4.[2] I provided a discussion of the information contained in the briefs of the litigants and *amicus* in *Carter* because it was an excellent example of the kind of behavior I had hypothesized to be of importance: interest groups making arguments about the preferences of the state legislature before members of a court whose job security is ultimately in the hands of that same state legislature. Here, I extend the discussion to the decision of the court itself.

While the litigants in the case focused on legal arguments, the NRDC, participating as *amicus*, devoted a sizable portion of its brief to the legislative intent, legislative history, and general competency of the state legislature. The decision of the court addressed the main issue in this case, whether or not the action of the Coastal Council, in denying a permit for the development of the land, constituted a taking of private property without adequate compensation. The court confined its attention primarily to the issue of the police power of the state and the appropriateness of the Coastal Council's action in this instance. The majority opinion held, in part, that:

> Controlling and restricting the filling of wetlands is clearly within the scope of the State's police power, as the legislature enacted the Coastal Zone Management Act

in response to its recognition of the detrimental effect the uncontrolled use of coastal wetlands would have on the public welfare.[3]

The court clearly was concerned about the impact that its decision would have on the public as well, citing lengthy passages from the Coastal Zone Management Act to buttress the concern of the legislature for the public good, and the competency of the legislature in passing such legislation to protect wetlands for future use. Such issues were not addressed by either litigant in this case; they were however the crux of the argument provided by the NRDC as *amicus*. The court did not wholly neglect to discuss the arguments forwarded by the litigants but did devote the vast majority of the space in their opinion to the issues brought up by *amicus*, dealing with the potential impact on the public, as well as the intent and expertise of the state legislature.

While *Carter* is an excellent example of a South Carolina state high court decision that mirrors the arguments provided by *amici*, it is not the only example. Other state supreme courts, where different selection mechanisms are used, have acted in similar fashion. In *State v. Gerhardstein*,[4] the Wisconsin supreme court was asked to decide whether the Equal Protection rights of individuals committed to mental health facilities were violated when those facilities administered psychotropic medication to them against their will. The petitioner, the state of Wisconsin, made six arguments: four that addressed the issue of mootness, one that the court of appeals was constitutionally precluded from making findings of fact, and one that habeas corpus was not an available remedy. In reply, the respondents, a state-employed physician and the Wisconsin Department of Health and Social Services, made five arguments: two that the case was moot, one that the court lacked personal jurisdiction, and two that the Wisconsin procedures were consistent with the Wisconsin and United States Constitutions. Both parties here relied heavily on threshold issues, suggesting that the case was improperly before the supreme court.

There were four *amicus* briefs filed in this case by the Wisconsin Psychiatric Association, the State Medical Society of Wisconsin, and the Wisconsin Coalition for Advocacy, and a fourth that was signed by the National Mental Health Association, National Mental Health Consumers Association, and the Mental Health Association of Wisconsin. The *amici* were more focused in the arguments that they provided, with two actors making two arguments in their brief, while the two other briefs contained three primary arguments. Consistent across briefs, whichever side they supported, was a commitment to two primary issues: (1) Whether the law passed by the Wisconsin legislature violated the patients' equal protection rights, and (2) the impact that allowing this practice to continue would ultimately have on the rights of the incompetent in the state as well as the larger ramifications on the privacy interests of its citizens. One of the three arguments forwarded by the Wisconsin Psychiatric Association was that:

"The Legislative policy of Wisconsin with respect to the administration of medication to involuntarily committed individuals meets the standards of the united states supreme court [*sic*] and recognizes the realities of medical practice."[5] The State Medical Society of Wisconsin supported a similar position, arguing that: "The legislature properly determined that clinical rather than judicial judgment is appropriate for determining involuntarily committed individuals' best medical interests."[6]

The Wisconsin Coalition for Advocacy, taking the opposite position, used a different tactic, choosing instead to alert the justices of the potential impact on the public if they were to uphold the Wisconsin legislature's efforts. They argued that:

> Upholding the right to consent to medications unless the person is incompetent or an emergency exists and upholding the requirement of a judicial determination of incompetence will not cause substantial disruptions in the treatment of committed psychiatric patients.[7]

The Coalition attempted to inform the Court of the impact on the medical community, and ultimately on health care delivery to the public. It was a direct appeal to the Court to uphold the court of appeals' decision to strike the legislatively mandated treatment provisions as unconstitutional on equal protection grounds.

In its opinion, the Wisconsin Supreme Court agreed with the Coalition and upheld the decision of the court of appeals. Rejecting the arguments made primarily by the petitioners, that the case was moot, the Court reasoned:

> Even if the case were moot as to the named persons, however, it would qualify for consideration, in that societal treatment of involuntarily committed individuals is an issue of great public importance...[8]

The court, having brushed aside the mootness argument, noting the societal importance of this issue, went on at length discussing the manner in which these medications were administered to patients. It recognized that, not only were they administered without consent, patients were not even informed of potential side effects, in stark contrast to the treatment of voluntarily committed psychiatric patients. They also picked up on the argument forwarded by the *amicus* Coalition regarding the impact on the health care delivery system, suggesting that informing patients of the side effects of the drugs had been shown to improve results. They went further, arguing that even if the decision did interfere with medical professionals doing their jobs, "Constitutional guarantees may not be replaced by professional judgment, and their protection and enforcement cannot be considered to be judicial interference."[9] The court was making both cases: Not only was there a benefit to the stoppage of current practices, even if there was no benefit, and instead a hindrance to the health care profession, that inconvenience was not sufficiently important to warrant the abrogation of constitutional rights.

This discussion shows that, at least in these instances, the body of the decision of the court takes on a character similar to the briefs filed in the case. This does show that it is not unheard of for courts to adopt, if not the exact wording, then at least the broad rationale and justification offered by *amici* when rendering their decisions. More to the point, in this chapter I seek to understand whether or not the courts are more receptive to particular arguments, and if it matters who is making those arguments to the court. I expect that, in fact, who makes the arguments to the court, and their status in the instant case—petitioner, respondent, or *amicus*—will be determinative in who ultimately prevails on the merits.

In the remainder of this chapter, I briefly review the major theories of judicial decision making and offer justification for employing the strategic theory of decision making to understand the behavior of state supreme court justices. I then lay out the models of state supreme court decision making and discuss the results from the data used to animate these models, drawing conclusions about the behavior of state supreme court justices.

## THEORIES OF JUDICIAL DECISION MAKING

There are three primary theories that have been applied to the decision making of judges: Legal, Attitudinal, and Strategic. These models, for the most part, have been directed at the behavior of justices on the United States Supreme Court. My focus is on the behavior of state supreme court justices, and as a result, the discussion that follows will lay out the general outlines of the attitudinal and strategic theories, with an emphasis on the application of the strategic theory of decision making to state supreme court justices.

### The Attitudinal Model

Proponents of the attitudinal model insist that the Supreme Court decides cases "...in light of the facts of the case vis-à-vis the ideological attitudes and values of the justices."[10] By this account, ideologically conservative justices will cast conservative votes and ideologically liberal judges will cast liberal votes.

There are two assumptions that are crucial to the attitudinal model. The first is that Supreme Court justices are appointed for life. As a result, they cannot, save for the most exceptional of circumstances, be removed from their posts. Additionally, as members of the Supreme Court, there is no higher court to which their decisions can be appealed, possibly leading to reversal. They are the final word on legal matters in this country. The attitudinalists suggest that these two institutional characteristics allow justices the freedom to decide cases based solely on their personal attitudes with little concern for the possible ramifications. In fact, they assume that, as impeachment of Supreme Court justices is extremely rare, there is no reason for justices to worry about removal.

It is important to keep the attitudinal model in its proper perspective. It is offered as an explanation for the behavior of Supreme Court justices. Not even the most ardent supporter of the attitudinal model would suggest that it serves as an adequate paradigm for understanding the behavior of inferior judges, either at the federal or state level. The fact that the judges on Circuit Courts of Appeal and District Courts are open to having their decisions appealed to higher courts prevents them from voting their sincere policy preferences given the facts of the case before them. State supreme court justices are similarly constrained as their federal counterparts but are doubly hampered from voting their preferences by the fact that the vast majority of them must face reelection on a regular basis. As a result, the attitudinal model is inappropriate for my purposes here: to better understand the behavior of state supreme court justices.

A more appropriate approach to explain the voting behavior of justices on state supreme courts is to adopt the strategic model of judicial decision making. With such an approach, I can account for institutional constraints on state supreme court justices that hinder their ability to obtain their most preferred policy preferences.

### The Strategic Model

In contrast to the attitudinal model, the strategic model posits that justices are not unconstrained actors with the ability to vote their sincere preferences. The general model does not suggest that justices pursue any particular goal or set of goals. It does hold that whatever the goals of justices—making good law, reelection, or policy—they are not free to vote their sincere preferences. I argue that policy is a primary goal of state supreme court justices. Therefore, they cannot pursue policy without considering the possible ramifications of their decisions both on the ultimate position that policy will take, but also on the legitimacy of the court itself.[11] Proponents of the model who adopt policy as a goal of justices suggest that, in order for justices to see their policy preferences remain as law, they must be cognizant of the policy preferences and potential actions that other political actors (both internal and external to the Court) may take that will ultimately shape the final face of the law.[12]

The basic assumptions of the strategic account are straightforward. Justices have goals, and most scholars that adopt strategic arguments suggest that their leading goal is policy. Justices behave strategically to obtain these policy goals. They do not simply vote their preferences when deciding cases as attitudinalists suggest. Despite the lack of accountability to a higher court or the fear of removal from their seat on the court, they are still aware that policy is not solely the result of their decisions alone. Other actors influence how the law is ultimately constructed. This ties in with the final assumption of the strategic account, which is that justices account for the institutional environment. Put simply, they understand who can impact policy and behave in ways to maximize their position in light of the power of those other actors.

Those who have adopted strategic models of judicial decision making have focused overwhelmingly on the United States Supreme Court.[13] Despite this emphasis on the Supreme Court, the strategic model is even more powerful from a theoretical perspective when it is focused on the behavior of justices on lower courts. In particular, the strategic model is the most appropriate theoretical approach to take when analyzing the behavior of state supreme court justices, where they are constrained both by the possibility of review by a higher court as well as concerns over their electoral security.

## STRATEGIC BEHAVIOR AND STATE SUPREME COURT JUSTICES

While there is still some substantial debate about the behavior of justices on the Supreme Court, and whether the attitudinal or strategic approach provides greater insight into how justices decide cases, the strategic model of decision making may be the more appropriate approach to take when analyzing state supreme court justices. State supreme court justices are limited in their ability to vote their sincere policy preferences by two critical constraints: their decisions are subject to review by a higher court, and they are not appointed to their positions for life. They must always be cognizant of the possibility that the decisions that they hand down will be appealed and subsequently reviewed by the Supreme Court.

Students of the courts are well aware, even though the likelihood that any individual decision of a state supreme court will be heard by the Supreme Court is low, the possibility exists for review, and that should serve to temper state supreme court justices from voting their pure policy preferences in all cases. This should continue to be so despite the decline in the size of the Supreme Court's docket. That state supreme court justices are electorally accountable to some constituency, whether directly to the public or indirectly, through the governor or state legislature, will also limit the likelihood that they will vote their strict policy preferences.

Instead, state supreme court justices will account for the institutional setting, evaluating the likelihood that their decision will be appealed to the Supreme Court, whether it will be accepted for review and overturned. State supreme court justices will also concern themselves with other actors who have the ability to shape the outlines of policy handed down by the court, including other members of the court, the state legislature, the governor, the relevant state agencies, and ultimately the public.

They will also be mindful of the possible electoral consequences of their decisions. They will make calculations about the salience of the case before them to the relevant actors with the power to remove them from office. With those estimates of the importance of a particular case, or set of cases, to those particular actors, state supreme court justices must make calculations about the probability that an adverse ruling will result in actions by those actors that will ultimately lead to the loss of their seat on the bench. This could take a number of forms, including concerted grassroots efforts by members of the public, campaigns by powerful interest groups, or even efforts by other governmental actors to oust judges in subsequent elections.

Because justices are interested in seeing the law mirror their policy preferences as closely as possible while at the same time avoiding electoral pitfalls, they will be motivated to acquire information about the potential consequences of their decisions. This makes the role of *amici curiae* at the state level all the more crucial. *Amici* serve as an important source of information to justices that allows them to pursue their policy and reelection goals effectively. Assuming that *amici* participate to provide information to justices that they might not otherwise get from the briefs submitted by litigants, it is critical to look at the role of those briefs in analyzing the decision making of state supreme court justices, and whether or not they do indeed behave in a strategic fashion.

As a result of their desire for both policy and electoral success, the behavior of state supreme court justices is best understood by adopting a strategic approach. While continuing to trumpet the attitudinal model as the most appropriate theoretical framework for understanding the voting behavior of Supreme Court justices, it is unlikely that even the most ardent supporters of this approach would argue that it applies to justices on state high courts. They are not free to vote their policy preferences and must pay attention to their institutional environment in which they make decisions. In the following section, I offer a model of state supreme court decision making that takes a strategic approach and focuses explicitly on the importance of the arguments contained in the briefs filed by litigants and *amici curiae*.

## A MODEL OF STATE SUPREME COURT DECISION MAKING

As I have maintained throughout this work, a strategic approach will be most useful in understanding the decision making of state supreme court justices. However, where others using such an approach have focused on the specific role of other institutional actors, here I focus on the importance of information provided by actors participating in the legal process, and how the institutional context is important in understanding the influence of that information on the behavior of state supreme court justices.[14]

This strategic model of judicial decision-making stresses the importance of two institutional features distinctive to the states: (1) judicial selection mechanisms, and (2) whether the state provides for direct public involvement in policy through the ballot initiative. Such mechanisms, it is expected, will influence the behavior of state supreme court justices in predictable ways. As the analysis of interest group behavior in the previous chapter shows, the institutional setting is correlated with expected patterns of behavior by groups. Similar results are expected by justices in state high courts.

This model for strategic behavior for state supreme court justices is predicated on the idea that information is crucial for them to achieve their goals. As a result, I argue that certain types of information will be of greater use to justices than others, and those litigants and *amici* that provide that information will enjoy greater success. Not only do I expect that the information provided by litigants and *amici* will be important for understanding case outcomes, but the identity of the party will be important as well. The degree of success achieved by these aforementioned actors is tempered by the institutional environment—what selection mechanisms are used and whether the state has the ballot initiative.

## Actors and Arguments

Information is critical for state supreme court justices, and the discussion of data on information contained in the litigant and *amicus* briefs in the previous chapter suggests that interest groups participate in distinctly different ways than other actors. Here I argue that, not only does the information provided to state supreme court justices matter when it comes to case outcomes, but the source of that information is critical as well. Whether it is received from the petitioner, respondent, or *amicus* is important. In addition, the actual identity of the party making the argument is expected to be crucial in understanding who prevails on the merits.

Certain arguments and information provided by litigants will be of greater use to state supreme court justices in certain institutional settings. Strategic, policy-seeking justices will want information that informs them of the possible actions of actors with the ability to influence the ultimate state of policy and who can exert electoral power over them. However, I begin by addressing the arguments made by the direct litigants in a case. The following hypotheses are directly related to the likelihood of success of the litigants as a result of the arguments made in their briefs.

***Hypothesis 13:*** *In states where state supreme court justices are accountable to the public (partisan, non-partisan, and merit), the more policy arguments made by petitioners, the more likely they are to win on the merits.*

***Hypothesis 14:*** *In states where state supreme court justices are accountable to other state actors (governor or state legislature), the more institutional arguments made by petitioners, the more likely they are to win on the merits.*

***Hypothesis 15:*** *In states where state supreme court justices are accountable to the public (partisan, non-partisan, and merit), the more policy arguments made by respondents, the less likely petitioners are to win on the merits.*

***Hypothesis 16:*** *In states where state supreme court justices are accountable to other state actors (governor or state legislature), the more institutional arguments made by respondents, the less likely petitioners are to win on the merits.*

The effect of arguments is expected to be cumulative. As a result, the support of *amici* should influence the outcome of a case. Scholars have shown that the presence of *amici* before the Supreme Court influences the likelihood that the justices will accept a case for review, and I expect that where an *amicus* supports the petitioner, it should serve as a signal to the court that there is additional support for that side in the case.[15] I extend this finding, suggesting that when justices are electorally accountable, interest group support of a litigant may influence the behavior of justices deciding cases on the merits.

***Hypothesis 17:*** *As the number of* amici *in support of the petitioner increases, the likelihood that the petitioner will win increases.*

Not only do I expect that the presence of *amici* in support of the petitioner's position will increase the likelihood of success for the petitioner, but the identity of the parties making the arguments should influence case outcomes as well. Justices will draw conclusions about the reliability and veracity of the arguments made by *amici*, and the source of the information will matter to justices. Interest groups will be viewed differently than individuals, corporations, and governmental actors.

***Hypothesis 18:*** *Interest group support of the petitioner as* amici *will increase the likelihood that the petitioner will win more than when other actors participating as* amici *support the petitioner's position.*

Not only will distinctions between the types of actors be important to state supreme court justices, I argue that differences between interest groups will be important to justices. An argument made by a locally based interest group will be viewed differently than one made by a national organization. Local groups are more likely to monitor the decisions of the court on a regular basis than national groups, and are the most likely actors to begin initiative efforts or campaigns to unseat justices. Also, these local groups are expected to participate before that court on at least a semi-regular basis, whereas national groups are more likely to participate infrequently in any given state, instead participating in only those cases that serve their goals. Moreover, local groups will be more well versed in the issue currently under consideration by the court. They have a more proximate connection to the issue, and being located in that state, will be able to understand the facts of the issue as well as the social, economic, and political ramifications relating to the case. Therefore, they will be in a more advantageous position and will be better able to relate relevant information to the justices. State supreme court justices should be aware of this as well and are going to be more inclined to also be able to make distinctions between those groups that have the ability, and possibly the inclination, to mount efforts to unseat justices from the court or begin efforts to overturn their decisions, either through influencing other institutions of government, or the public through the ballot initiative.

***Hypothesis 19:*** *When the petitioner is supported by local groups, the petitioner is more likely to win than when the petitioner is supported by nationally based groups.*

The arguments made by *amici* will likely influence the outcome of the case as well. Justices cannot afford to ignore the information that is provided to them by *amici*, and it is quite likely that the information provided in *amicus* briefs alerts justices to the ramifications of their decisions. Information gathering is quite costly for groups, and it is unlikely that they would purposely provide information they know to be incorrect, or to purposely mislead state supreme court justices. Their reputations as reliable sources of information would be seriously compromised if state supreme court justices were to learn that they had been provided with, and relied upon, false or intentionally misleading information.

***Hypothesis 20:*** *In states where state supreme court justices are more directly accountable to the public (partisan, non-partisan, and merit), the more policy arguments made by* amici *in support of the petitioner, the more likely the petitioner is to win on the merits.*

***Hypothesis 21:*** *In states where justices are accountable to other state actors (governor or state legislature), the more institutional arguments made by* amici, *the more likely the petitioner is to win on the merits.*

The information from *amici* should be viewed as more credible than that obtained from the direct litigants in a case. *Amicus* participation is voluntary and those who participate presumably have some degree of expertise on a particular issue. Therefore, their information should have a degree of credibility that litigants otherwise do not have. This is even more true for the participation of interest groups as *amici curiae*, who would be expected to have, not only access to the most reliable sources of information, but also the greatest incentive to provide that information to justices, taking care to avoid being viewed as an unreliable source of information.

## DATA AND METHODS

In order to evaluate these hypotheses, I construct models that focus on the actors in their capacities as information providers to the courts and what information they do provide to the justices. The arguments that litigants and *amici* provide in their briefs are hypothesized to be important factors in determining case outcomes. State supreme court justices must concern themselves with the political environment, and when confronted with multiple actors in support of a position, they desire information that alerts them to policy outcomes and about the possibility of electoral threats.

### Dependent Variables

The dependent and independent variables included in the general model are listed in Table 5.1. For the general models, the dependent variable is the direction of the courts' decision. The direction is coded as 1 if the court's decision is liberal, and 0 otherwise. I follow Harold Spaeth's coding scheme from the United States Supreme Court Database in determining whether a decision by a court is liberal or conservative. There were originally 637 cases in the original data set. However, numerous cases defy liberal/conservative classification. These include issue areas such as dissolution (divorce), taxation, and zoning issues. As a result, sixty-eight cases were removed from the final model.

### Independent Variables

The first independent variable is a measure of the ideological position of the state supreme court. The ideological position was calculated by taking the party identification of each justice, coded as 1 if Democrat and 0 if Republican. The party identification serves as a proxy for the ideological position of the justices. The median ideological position of each court was then calculated using these scores. This is not the most ideal measure for ideological position of the court, but in the absence of better measures, others have demonstrated that it is an acceptable strategy when conducting research on the decision making of state supreme court justices.[16]

In addition to a measure of the individual courts' median ideological position, it was also necessary to code for the ideological position of the public and other state level governmental actors in the states. Fortunately such measures are readily available for citizen and elite ideology.[17] However, the measures provided by Berry, et al. only cover the period until

Table 5.1
Variable Explanations for Probit Models

| | |
|---|---|
| **Dependent Variable:** | |
| **Direction of the Decision:** | Coded as 1 if Liberal decision, 0 Otherwise. |
| **Independent Variables:** | |
| **Court Ideology:** | Median ideological position of state supreme court. |
| **Citizen Ideology:** | Ideology score of the public in that state (Berry, et al 1998). |
| **Government Ideology:** | Ideology score of the elite in that state (Berry, et al. 1998). |
| **Petitioner Position:** | Coded as 1 if Petitioner supports liberal position, 0 Otherwise. |
| **Petitioner Policy (Institution):** | Number of Policy (Institution) arguments made by Petitioner. |
| **Respondent Policy (Institution):** | Number of Policy (Institution) arguments made by Respondent. |
| **Amicus Policy (Institution):** | Number of Policy (Institution) arguments made by *Amici.* |
| **Interest Group:** | Coded as 1 if Interest Group, 0 Otherwise. |
| **Local Group:** | Coded as 1 if Local Interest Group, 0 Otherwise. |
| **National Group:** | Coded as 1 if National Interest Group, 0 Otherwise. |
| **Business/Corporation:** | Coded as 1 if Business, 0 Otherwise. |
| **State/Government:** | Coded as 1 if State/Local Government, 0 Otherwise. |
| **Federal Government:** | Coded as 1 if Federal Government, 0 Otherwise. |

(continued)

**Table 5.1**
*(continued)*

| | |
|---|---|
| **Partisan:** | Coded as 1 if a Partisan selection state, 0 Otherwise. |
| **Non-Partisan:** | Coded as 1 if a Non-Partisan selection state, 0 Otherwise. |
| **Merit:** | Coded as 1 if a Merit selection state, 0 Otherwise. |
| **Gubernatorial:** | Coded as 1 if a Gubernatorial state, 0 Otherwise. |
| **Legislative:** | Coded as 1 if a Legislative appointment state, 0 Otherwise. |
| **Ballot Initiative:** | Coded as1 if an Initiative state, 0 Otherwise. |

1993. As a result, cases from 1994 and 1995 were not used in estimating the final model. Ultimately, 442 cases were included in the final model. With these measures of the ideological position of the state supreme court, the public, and the other governmental elites, I can evaluate the relationship between the arguments made by litigants and *amici* and their impact on judicial outcomes.

I coded the ideological direction of both the petitioner, coded as 1 if supporting the liberal position and 0 if supporting a conservative outcome. The position of the petitioner is important, in that I expect the court to uphold petitioners with whom they are ideologically aligned.

I also included variables to track the identity of the actors involved in the case. I identified the parties as corporations, state/government, or interest group for petitioners, respondents, and *amici curiae*. My expectation is that there will be differences in the level of success depending on the identity of the litigants, but also on the identity of the *amicus* in support of the litigants.

Variables representing the number, and category, or arguments made in the briefs of actors were included in the model. There are measures of the number of policy and institutional arguments made by petitioners, respondents, and *amici*. I expect that policy arguments will have a greater impact in states with the ballot initiative and where state supreme court justices are directly accountable to voters.

Lastly, I include dichotomous variables for the selection systems used by the states, covering partisan, non-partisan, merit, gubernatorial, and legislative appointment systems. The variable is coded as 1 if the state employs a particular selection system, and 0 otherwise. I also include a dichotomous variable for whether the state allows for the ballot initiative in the state, coded as 1 if the state allows public participation through the initiative, and 0 otherwise.

## RESULTS

With these variables I use two probit models to estimate the likelihood of a liberal outcome. In the policy model, I focus on policy arguments made by the various actors to evaluate the importance of the identities of actors in different institutional settings. In the institutions model, I focus on the institutional arguments made by the actors: petitioners, respondents, and *amici curiae*.

### Policy Model

The results of the policy model are reported in Table 5.2. The ideological position of the petitioner is signed in the expected direction and highly correlated with case outcomes. Where the petitioner supports the liberal position in the case, there is an increased probability of a liberal outcome in the case. This is consistent with the conventional wisdom suggesting that courts accept cases for review that they are interested in overturning. Courts are generally not likely to review cases that they wish to affirm on the merits and are more likely to engage in error correction strategies, generally taking those cases from lower courts that are out of line with the direction of the state supreme court.

There is no statistically significant correlation between the ideological position of the court and the probability of a liberal outcome. This is not particularly surprising for a number of reasons. The first has to do with the measure itself. When discussing the independent variables used in these models, I made note of the problems associated with using the party identification of the justices as a surrogate for the liberalism of the court. It is an imprecise measure at best, but at this point it is sufficient.

The absence of a statistically significant relationship between the Court variable and the ideological direction of the decision, despite the enumerated problems associated with the measure itself, is not wholly unexpected from a theoretical perspective. I expect state supreme court justices to behave strategically, and a significant correlation between the ideological position of the court and the direction of the decision would be inconsistent with the expectation of strategic voting behavior on the part of state supreme court justices. Measures of the ideology of U.S. Supreme Court justices have proven to be quite robust, at least for cases involving civil liberties cases.[18] However, this is readily explained by the fact that

**Table 5.2**
**Parameter Estimates for Probit Model—Policy**

| **Independent Variables** | **Parameter Estimates** (Standard Errors in Parentheses) |
|---|---|
| Court | -0.182 (0.524) |
| Citizen Ideology | 0.392 (0.225) |
| Government Ideology | 0.297 (0.428) |
| Petitioner Position | 0.403 (0.119)*** |
| **Petitioner Policy Arguments** | |
| Group | -0.065 (0.178) |
| State/Government | -0.118 (0.108) |
| Business | 0.045 (0.078) |
| **Respondent Policy Arguments** | |
| Group | -0.659 (0.359) |
| State/Government | -0.213 (0.084)*** |
| Business | 0.058 (0.069) |
| **Amicus Policy Arguments for Petitioner** | |
| Local Group | -0.033 (0.007) |
| National Group | 0.023 (0.017) |
| State/Government | 0.115 (0.054)* |
| Business | -0.011 (0.017) |
| **Amicus Policy Arguments for Respondent** | |
| Local Group | 0.015 (0.001) |
| National Group | -0.037 (0.036) |
| State/Government | -0.109 (0.040)*** |
| Business | 0.024 (0.044) |
| **Institutional Features** | |
| Partisan | -0.484 (0.245)** |
| Non-Partisan | -0.185 (0.330) |
| Merit | -0.098 (0.271) |
| Gubernatorial | -0.644 (0.327)** |
| Ballot Initiative | 0.050 (0.166) |
| Constant | 0.145 (0.565) |

Likelihood Ratio $\chi^2$: 64.58
Prob > $\chi^2$: 0.000
Log Likelihood: -362.042
Number of Observations: 442

*Significant at $p< .10$
**Significant at $p< .05$
***Significant at $p< .01$

U.S. Supreme Court justices have no need to worry about reelection; they are appointed for life and enjoy more latitude in their ability to make decisions in line with their policy preferences exactly because they do not have the institutional constraints operating on them that state jurists confront.

Moreover, there does not appear to be a statistically significant relationship between citizen ideology or government ideology and the likelihood of success by the petitioner. Apparently, the court is little concerned about the relative position of those actors when making decisions. This may be because the vast majority of cases heard and decided by state supreme courts are not highly salient and therefore are not likely to engender a response. If one were to control for issue area, focusing on highly salient cases that had received substantial media attention, or were particularly important issues to the public or members of the state legislatures, the results may be quite different. It may also be that the court is not ideologically distant from these other actors, and therefore there is little reason to see divergence between the court and these other actors. Since they are accountable to the public, or to other institutions, it is logical to expect state supreme court justices to be ideologically proximate to the other branches or the public. These data certainly do not support the proposition that state supreme court justices behave strategically in response to the position of the public or other branches of state government.

Addressing the arguments made by the various actors before the courts, the results are intriguing. First, the identity of the petitioner appears not to have an impact on the decision of the court. I expected that status as a group, governmental entity, or business actor would increase the likelihood of success for petitioners. This is not supported by the data.

However, looking at the results of the information provided by respondents to the court, a slightly different picture emerges. While the group and business variables still do not achieve statistical significance, the state/government variable is negatively signed and significant at the .01 level. Where the state or other governmental actors make policy arguments on behalf of the respondent, the likelihood of the petitioner winning is decreased. Apparently, and not totally surprisingly, the arguments forwarded by the state or other governmental entities are more important to the court than those forwarded by other actors. This could be a result of a number of factors. Courts may view the expertise and ability of such actors to comment on policy outcomes as more credible than that presented by the other categories of actors.

This is borne out by the arguments forwarded by *amici*, both in support of the petitioner and the respondent. The policy variable in support of the petitioner is significant at .10 while the policy variable in support of the respondent is significant at the .01 level. They are signed in the expected directions as well. Policy arguments made by governmental actors acting as *amici curiae* in support of petitioners increases the probability of success for the petitioner, while policy arguments made by governmental actors in support of the respondent decreases the probability of success for the petitioners.

The institutional differences between the states provides an interesting image of the behavior of state supreme court justices. The partisan and gubernatorial variables are the only two that are significantly related to the likelihood of petitioner success, and negatively related at that. The ballot initiative is positively signed but is not significant. All of the variables are negatively signed, and it is difficult to understand why the probability of the petitioner winning decreases in partisan election states in particular. This may be due in part to some of the aspects specific to Alabama that were discussed in Chapter 4, and why the partisan election variable was not significant in those models. It is perhaps a bit easier to understand the gubernatorial variable results, as policy arguments are expected to be less influential in those states than in other states where state supreme court justices are directly accountable to the public.

The most compelling conclusion that can be taken from the data presented by the policy model is that when the state or other governmental actors participate on behalf of one of the litigants in a case, the arguments that they present have an impact on the outcome of cases. Judicial selection mechanisms also do not appear to be correlated in the predicted ways with the likelihood that the court will arrive at a liberal outcome.

### Institutions Model

I have also estimated the institutions model where the argument variables focus on the institutional arguments made by each of the various actors. The results are reported in Table 5.3. Once again, the position taken by the petitioner is highly correlated with the direction of the decision—where the petitioners support the liberal position, they are more likely to win regardless of judicial selection mechanism.

Again the court, citizen ideology, and government ideology variables are not significant in this model either. I offer the same possible explanation for this as I did for the policy model. State supreme court justices may just not care what the positions of these other actors are, choosing to vote more along their own policy preferences, than adjusting their votes in response to the ideology of other actors, even those with the power to affect the ultimate state of policy and the ability to remove them from office.

However, unlike the results in the Policy model, the state/government variables are not significant in this model. In fact, only when a group makes policy arguments when participating as petitioner and businesses participating as respondents are significant, and then only at the .10 level. None of the variables for *amici curiae* are significant either.

Table 5.3
**Parameter Estimates for Probit Model—Institutions**

| Independent Variables | Parameter Estimates (Standard Errors in Parentheses) |
|---|---|
| Court | -0.282 (0.519) |
| Citizen Ideology | 0.502 (0.388) |
| Government Ideology | 0.471 (0.602) |
| Petitioner Position | 0.407 (0.118)*** |
| **Petitioner Institutional Arguments** | |
| Group | -0.446 (0.271)* |
| State/Government | -0.045 (0.106) |
| Business | -0.112 (0.148) |
| **Respondent Institutional Arguments** | |
| Group | -0.022 (0.197) |
| State/Government | -0.143 (0.010) |
| Business | 0.284 (0.162)* |
| **Amicus Institutional Arguments for Petitioner** | |
| Local Group | -0.001 (0.012) |
| National Group | 0.028 (0.059) |
| State/Government | 0.130 (0.082) |
| Business | -0.049 (0.049) |
| **Amicus Institutional Arguments for Respondent** | |
| Local Group | 0.018 (0.020) |
| National Group | -0.097 (0.138) |
| State/Government | -0.100 (0.070) |
| Business | 0.022 (0.110) |
| **Institutional Features** | |
| Partisan | -0.426 (0.244)* |
| Non-Partisan | -0.174 (0.325) |
| Merit | -0.131 (0.267) |
| Gubernatorial | -0.683 (0.323)** |
| Ballot Initiative | 0.100 (0.164) |
| Constant | 0.188 (0.558) |

Likelihood Ratio $\chi^2$: 51.38
Prob > $\chi^2$: 0.0002
Log Likelihood: -368.64
Number of Observations: 442

*Significant at $p< .10$
**Significant at $p< .05$
***Significant at $p< .01$

Again, looking at the institutional variables, all of the variables are negatively signed, and again, only the partisan and gubernatorial variables are significant. The results suggest that despite selection system, and despite the arguments forwarded by virtually all actors, the probability of a liberal decision is not affected.

## CONCLUSION

There are a number of important conclusions to be drawn from the analysis in this chapter on the decision making of state supreme court justices. One of the central assumptions that I have made is that state supreme court justices behave strategically when making decisions. My purpose was to show that decisions of justices are interdependent—they account for the preferences and possible actions of other actors when deciding cases. The data presented here present a mixed portrait of decision making. The data suggest that only in limited circumstances do the arguments presented by certain actors matter when understanding the decisions of state supreme court justices.

These were not the results that I was expecting, and this causes me to pause and reconsider some of the assumptions regarding the behavior of state supreme court justices. The results from Chapter 4 suggest that interest groups do behave in strategic ways, presenting arguments to state supreme court justices in states with different selection mechanisms that they believe will be of use to those justices. Presumably, they do so because they believe that such arguments will influence the decisions of justices. If that is indeed their goal, it does not appear to be successful. This is not a trivial finding. Litigants and *amici* appear to be behaving in strategic ways, while state supreme court justices are not. Perhaps those participating in the courts are providing information for reasons other than to necessarily influence outcomes. It is also quite possible that this is a learning process that will take time for groups, and others, to become more sophisticated actors when providing information.

There are also methodological issues to be discussed that may have influenced the results here. First, the data set used included cases from all states. It would have been more desirable to estimate models for each state to capture the possible interaction effects between selection mechanism and the information provided by the litigants and *amici*. This was not feasible given the available data. The size of each of the individual state data sets were too small to obtain accurate parameter estimates.[19] Future analyses would include more data from individual states to estimate these models.

Additionally, I did not control for issue area in collecting these data. It is quite possible, and perhaps likely, that state supreme court justices would exhibit strategic behavior in particular issue areas such as abortion rights, death penalty, or criminal procedure. Future work should focus on cases in particular issue areas. This may be somewhat problematic, as *amicus* involvement may not be of sufficient magnitude in certain issue areas to estimate models. However, I feel that some of the more salient issues will draw substantial *amicus* participation to be able to analyze group and judicial behavior in those areas, particularly in states with highly professionalized interest group environments, and with large and diverse populations, leading to a wide variety of cases filtering up to state supreme courts.

## NOTES

1. Paul Reidinger. 1987. "The Politics of Judging." *ABA Journal* 73: 52.
2. *Carter v. South Carolina Coastal Council* (304 S.E. 2d 327, 1986).
3. *Carter,* pp. 5–6.
4. *State v. Gerhardstein* (416 N.W. 2d 883, 1987).
5. *Amicus* brief of the Wisconsin Psychiatric Association.
6. *Amicus* brief of the State Medical Society of Wisconsin.
7. *Amicus* brief of the Wisconsin Coalition for Advocacy.
8. *State,* p. 19.
9. *State,* p. 41.
10. Jeffrey A. Segal and Harold J. Spaeth. 1993. *The Supreme Court and the Attitudinal Model.* Cambridge: Cambridge University Press.
11. See e.g., Lee Epstein and Jack Knight. 1998. *The Choices Justices Make.* Washington: CQ Press.
12. Epstein and Knight, *The Choices Justices Make.*
13. William N. Eskridge Jr. 1991a. "Overriding Supreme Court Statutory Interpretation Decisions." *Yale Law Journal* 101: 331–417; William N. Eskridge Jr. 1991b. "Reneging on History?: Playing the Court/Congress/President Civil Rights Game." *California Law Review* 79: 613–84; Rafael Gely and Pablo Spiller. 1990. "A Rational Choice Theory of Supreme Court Statutory Decisions with Applications to the *State Farm* & *Grove City* Cases." *Journal of Law, Economics and Organization* 6: 263–300; Rafael Gely and Pablo Spiller. 1992. "The Political Economy of Supreme Court Constitutional Decisions: The Case of Roosevelt's Court Packing Plan." *International Review of Law and Economics* 12: 45–67; Jack Knight and Lee Epstein. 1996. "On the Struggle for Judicial Supremacy." *Law and Society Review* 30: 87–120; Epstein and Knight. *The Choices Justices Make;* Lee Epstein and Jack Knight. 1999. "Mapping Out the Strategic Terrain: The Informational Role of *Amici Curiae.*" In *Supreme Court Decision-Making: New Institutional Approaches,* eds. Howard Gillman and Cornell W. Clayton. Chicago: University of Chicago Press; Andrew Martin. 1998. *Strategy, and The Separation of Powers.* Unpublished doctoral dissertation, Washington University, St. Louis.
14. Melinda Gann-Hall. 1992. "Electoral Politics and Strategic Voting in State Supreme Courts." *Journal of Politics* 54: 427–46; Melinda Gann-Hall. 1995. "Justices as Representatives: Elections and Judicial Politics in the American States." *American Politics Quarterly* 23: 485–503; Melinda Gann-Hall and Paul Brace. 1989. "Order in the Courts: A Neo-Institutional Approach to Judicial Consensus." *Western Political*

*Quarterly* 42: 391–407; Melinda Gann-Hall and Paul Brace. 1992. "Toward an Integrated Model of Judicial Voting Behavior. *American Politics Quarterly* 20: 147–168.

15. Gregory A. Caldeira and John R. Wright. 1988. "Organized Interests and Agenda Setting in the U.S. Supreme Court." *American Political Science Review* 82: 1109–27.

16. Hall and Brace, "Toward an Integrated Model of Judicial Voting Behavior;" Donald R. Songer and Susan J. Tabrizi. 1999. "The Religious Right in Court: the Decision Making of Christian Evangelicals in State Supreme Courts." *Journal of Politics* 61 (2): 507–26.

17. William D. Berry, Evan J. Ringquist, Richard C. Fording, and Russell L. Hanson. "Measuring Citizen and Government Ideology in the American States, 1960–93." *American Journal of Political Science* 42 (1): 327–48.

18. Jeffrey A. Segal and Albert Cover. 1989. "Ideological Values and the Votes of U.S. Supreme Court Justices." *American Political Science Review* 83: 557–65; but see also Lee Epstein and Carol Mershon. 1996. "Measuring Political Preferences." *American Journal of Political Science* 40: 261–94.

19. J. Scott Long. 1997. *Regression Models for Categorical and Limited Dependent Variables.* Thousand Oaks, CA: Sage Publications.

# CHAPTER 6

# Conclusion

From the outset, I have assumed that state supreme court justices behave strategically when making decisions. This, along with the assumption that interest groups are strategic actors, serves as the foundation for the theoretical discussion and motivates the entire work. In addition, I assume that state supreme court justices desire information that will allow them to reach decisions resulting in outcomes that are as close to their preferred goals as possible.[1] The *amicus* briefs filed by interest groups are one of the primary sources from which they can obtain this information. I argue that the ability of state supreme court justices to vote their sincere preferences is constrained by the institutional environment in which they operate. Unlike federal judges who serve for life, state supreme court judges are elected, consistently confronting reelection concerns. I argue that these electoral constraints, coupled with the active role in the policy-making process available to the public in a number of states, result in interest groups providing information to state supreme court justices that they feel will be of use to those justices. In response, state supreme court justices will behave strategically, using the information provided to them to reach their policy and reelection goals when making decisions.

In this chapter, I bring together the empirical findings on the behavior of state supreme court justices and those actors participating before them, place these results within the larger context of the field of judicial politics, and demonstrate how this work adds to that research tradition. I return to the basic question of whether, and to what degree, institutions constrain the behavior of actors in the legal process. I discuss why it is important to understand the role of institutions in ordering the behavior of actors in the legal process, focusing primarily on state supreme court justices and interest groups. I then discuss some of the more significant empirical findings and how they support my hypotheses. Finally, I turn my attention to the implications of this work, possible extensions of this research, and how it contributes to a greater understanding of interest group participation in the courts and judicial decision making.

## THE IMPORTANCE OF INSTITUTIONS

I provide analyses of both the litigants participating in state supreme courts and the justices sitting on those courts. The purpose of this research is to demonstrate that it is important to understand the role played by the institutional structure and how it affects the decision making of the actors involved. In this section, I review these findings for actors and justices and synthesize the principal results.

### Litigants, *Amici Curiae*, and their Briefs

The analysis of strategic behavior in state supreme courts begins with the litigants and *amici curiae* that participate in those courts. I assume that interest groups are strategic actors who pursue the dual goals of group maintenance and policy attainment. Participation before the courts is one method used by groups to achieve these goals. Specifically, filing *amicus curiae* briefs allows groups to become involved in issues that will be of interest to their membership and give the group an opportunity to provide the information that they feel will be of the greatest use to state supreme court justices. Groups provide information with the expectation that it will be used by the justices on the court, possibly leading to favorable policy outcomes for the group and its members. I argue that interest groups are aware of the goals of state supreme court justices and will tailor their briefs to account for institutional constraints, making arguments that will allow justices to achieve their own goals as well.

I compare the information provided by *amici curiae* to that provided by both petitioners and respondents. My primary expectation is that interest groups are strategic actors and have the legal and financial resources to provide information to state supreme court justices that will allow them to achieve their goals. Other actors are not expected to have the inclination, or ability, to effectively develop a long-term strategy to pursue policy directly through the courts. Not only do I expect differences in the behavior of actors when participating as *amici curiae*, I suggest that the character of the involvement in the legal process is critical.

The results largely confirm these hypotheses. In four of the seven states, *amici curiae* include proportionately more policy arguments in their briefs than both petitioners and respondents. However, in only three states do *amici* make proportionately more institutional arguments than the litigants. One of those states is South Carolina, where justices are elected directly by the state legislature, and the difference between the mean number of institutional arguments by *amici* and the litigants is quite large. For South Carolina, where I expected the differences to be manifested most clearly, the data support my expectations. This suggests that the accepted role and purpose of *amici curiae* in the legal process is markedly different from those who are parties to the case. I expected litigants and *amici* in the gubernatorial state, New Jersey, to mimic the behavior of actors in South Carolina. However, the data do not support this hypothesis. Clearly the fact that justices are accountable to the legislature, and not the governor, results in a marked difference in the behavior of litigants and *amici curiae.*

Given the somewhat mixed results, I employed a multivariate approach to gain more purchase on the role of institutions in ordering the behavior of legal actors. However, I further extended the hypotheses to encompass not only the differences between litigants and *amici*, but also differences among individuals, businesses, government, and interest groups. The results of the multivariate analysis are more convincing. When local (state level) interest groups participate in cases as *amici curiae*, the likelihood of additional arguments, both institutional and policy, is increased. For no other actor participating as *amici curiae* does the likelihood of additional arguments increase. This says a great deal about the efforts of local interest groups in particular. Local groups are more likely than national organizations to have information about potential policy outcomes. They are more involved on a daily basis with the pursuit of policy and will be better informed about the issues than other actors. Also, participation by governmental actors or businesses as *amici curiae* does not increase the likelihood of additional arguments about policy or the preferences of other institutions.

One of the findings of this research that was not expected, but is worthy of note: When governmental actors participate as litigants, the likelihood of additional institutional arguments is increased. Though not explicitly hypothesized, this is not wholly surprising. When these actors participate, they are motivated to comment either on their own preferences, or those of other governmental actors. It is not clear why they are more willing to make such arguments when they are litigants, and not when they participate as *amici curiae.*

In addition to government entities, only local interest groups participating as respondents has an effect on the number of institutional arguments in a given case. I am at loss to explain why it is that local groups would be likely to include more institutional arguments when they are respondents but not do so when they are participating as petitioners. I suggested that actors are more constrained in making certain arguments when they are involved as litigants. It may be that when they are participating as respondents they are able to respond to arguments forwarded by petitioners that implicate the preferences of government actors. Also, interest groups are infrequent participants as litigants. Most litigants are individuals, government, and businesses. When local groups are respondents in state supreme courts, it may be that they are opposed by government actors that have appealed from a lower court decision. As a result, they may be responding to those arguments forwarded by the government actors, implicating the preferences and potential responses of state-level institutions to the decision of the court.

When business actors are involved in litigation, the likelihood of additional policy arguments increases—the only actor for which this occurs. I submit that businesses may be motivated to include information about the possible economic consequences of a decision by the court. By that I mean that a business may use the potential for negative economic impact as a tool to influence the courts. I do not expect that individual businesses consider the use of the courts as an integral part of their business philosophy. It is more likely the case that businesses belong to associations that represent particular business or economic sectors. Associations will serve the interests of its constituent members, attempting to obtain favorable policy through the courts, as well as through other methods. Here the data suggest that the participation of individual businesses as litigants does increase the likelihood of additional policy arguments.

Overall, the results from Chapter 4 regarding the information included in the briefs of litigants and *amici curiae* support my hypotheses. In particular, the data offer strong evidence that at least local interest groups behave strategically, including information in their briefs that will likely be of use to strategic, policy-minded state supreme court justices.

## Institutions and Information

The discussion above makes clear the differences in behavior by actors and how their status as litigant or *amicus* affects behavior. In this section, I focus on the results from Chapter 4 that illuminate the role institutions play in ordering the information found in the briefs filed by litigants and *amici curiae*. I expected that in states where state supreme court justices are directly accountable to one of the coordinate branches of state government, *amici curiae* would make more arguments about the preferences of those actors. Conversely, where justices face reelection campaigns before the voters of their respective states, the *amici* should make more policy arguments, informing the court of the impact of the decision of the court. The results for both of these expectations are intriguing.

South Carolina requires that state supreme court justices regularly face the members of the state legislature to retain their seats on the court. I argue that state legislatures have greater capacity to alter the decisions of state supreme courts than either the governor or the public, especially through their ability to overturn statutory decisions of the court through legislation. Consequently, *amici curiae* should provide information about the preferences of the state legislature and what actions they may take in response to the decisions of the court. The multivariate analysis generally supports this expectation. In all systems, save for Alabama (a state where justices are chosen via partisan elections) *amici* are less likely to include arguments about the other state level institutions than *amici* in South Carolina. I expected *amici* in New Jersey, where justices are chosen by the governor, to make institutional arguments with relatively the same frequency as in South Carolina, but that was not the case. The greater ability of legislatures to alter court decisions may account for the fact that *amici* are not making institutional arguments in large numbers in New Jersey.

Alabama also stands out as a state where the behavior of *amici* does not comport with expectations. There is a long history of lax regulation of lobbying of the state legislature. As a result, it is certainly plausible to expect that interest groups use their resources to pursue policy primarily through the legislature and not the courts. It is possible that groups simply do not treat participation in state supreme courts as crucial to the attainment of their policy and maintenance goals as groups in other states.

The effect of institutions on policy arguments provides a slightly different picture. In the non-partisan and merit selection states, *amici* are more likely to make policy arguments than in South Carolina. Where justices are more accountable to the electorate, *amici* address more policy arguments in their briefs. Again, *amici* in Alabama, the partisan election state, do not behave significantly differently from *amici* in South Carolina.

The results for petitioners and respondents in the institutions model did not suggest that institutional mechanisms influenced their behavior. However, litigants mirror the behavior of *amici* in the amount of policy arguments made. Petitioners and respondents both make more policy arguments in non-partisan and merit selection states. This suggests that there may be some strategic behavior on the part of litigants.

One consistent finding throughout is the lack of a statistically significant relationship in the expected direction for the ballot initiative. It has been argued that the initiative, a device that allows the public to become involved directly in policy making, may influence judicial behavior.[2] If justices view it as a constraint, then strategic, sophisticated groups should understand this and tailor their briefs accordingly. The data clearly do not support this expectation. As I suggested in Chapter 4, it is a mechanism that is infrequently used, and this may be why state supreme court justices do not view it as a constraint on their behavior. If this is so, it is not surprising that interest groups do not respond to it when constructing their briefs.

The conclusions to draw from the analysis in Chapter 4 are primarily that institutions do appear to play some role in the behavior of important legal actors. Interest groups do understand the institutional environment in which they are operating and make arguments that they feel will be of the greatest use to state supreme court justices in achieving their goals.

### Electoral Accountability and the Behavior of State Supreme Court Justices

The data from Chapter 4 are fairly compelling. The results support the conclusion that interest groups behave strategically, accounting for the institutional structure in composing their briefs. However, the results in Chapter 5 are less conclusive. If state supreme court justices are strategic actors looking to maximize their chances for reelection and the attainment of policy outcomes as close to their preferences as possible, then it is logical to expect them to make use of the information provided to them in the briefs filed by litigants. The information in the briefs filed by litigants is one of the primary sources of information about the legal issues involved in a case, the potential ramifications of that case on the law, and the ultimate state of policy.

As Chapter 4 showed, groups do appear to behave strategically when participating as *amici*. This means that justices are getting the kinds of information that will assist them in achieving their policy and reelection goals. The question regarding the importance of this information provided by *amici* is whether or not it is put to use by state supreme court justices and whether it manifests itself in the decision making of the justices.

The results from Chapter 5 do not suggest that the arguments made by litigants and *amici curiae* influence the behavior of state supreme court justices. Few of the independent variables included in the model to explain the decisions of the courts are statistically significant. I would not take these results as evidence that the strategic model is inappropriate for understanding the behavior of state supreme court justices, but it does not provide much support for that model either. This approach to the decision making of state supreme court justices should not be interpreted to mean that the information provided by *amici* is not used by the court. My focus with this portion of the research is on judicial outcomes. It may prove to be useful in future analyses to employ an approach similar to that used by Spriggs and Wahlbeck, performing content analysis on the opinions of the courts to see if specific arguments made in *amicus* briefs make their way into the final decision on the merits.[3]

The results of this chapter, while they do not support the strategic model of state supreme court behavior, should not be taken as conclusive. Future approaches to the decision making of state supreme court justices should employ more precise measures of the preferences of those justices.

In addition, one of the limitations of these data is that they are not drawn from a specific issue area. Future work should focus on specific areas in which the use of measures of judicial preferences are most likely to be appropriate, such as civil liberties and criminal procedure.

## IMPLICATIONS

Though it is often said, and perhaps to the point of being cliché, this work attempts to fill an as yet largely unrecognized gap in the field of judicial politics. It is an initial attempt to better understand the role that institutions play in demarcating the boundaries constraining the behavior of actors in state supreme courts. However, this project also speaks to those interested in the study of courts, interest groups, and state politics. The bulk of the work by scholars in this field focuses on the decision-making process, generally disregarding state courts. Most research, with some exceptions,[4] has ignored the role of legal actors and the importance of legal argumentation. These findings suggest that there are differences in the arguments made by litigants and *amici*, and that institutions play a role in understanding the information contained in the briefs filed by these actors.

This research also adds more support to the argument that in order to understand the behavior of political actors, it is critical to understand the institutional structure that defines the environment in which the decisions of those elites are made. This work rests primarily on this assumption that institutions are central to an understanding of the behavior of political actors. Institutions limit the ability of political actors to make decisions that are congruent with their preferences. The results show that these actors, at least *amici curiae*, are constrained by their environment and adapt to achieve their goals within these limits.

State supreme courts have long been neglected by judicial scholars, and it is an area of study in need of increased consideration. This lack of attention is a result of a number of factors, but prominent among them is that state supreme courts simply have not been viewed as being as important as the U.S. Supreme Court or other federal courts. The policy-making authority of the Supreme Court certainly outweighs that of any other court, but with the docket of the Supreme Court declining in recent years, more scholars have been turning their attention to lower federal courts, state supreme courts, and most recently to the comparative study of courts.

Another reason for the paucity of research in the area has to do with the lack of data on these courts. However, as state governments have become more professionalized in recent years, this has resulted in more accurate and extensive record keeping. With the advent of the Internet, and the proliferation of online data sources, our ability to focus on these data for the purpose of conducting rigorous research projects has greatly increased.

This work also should cause some reconsideration of the suitability of the attitudinal or strategic models to assess the behavior of state supreme court justices. Segal and Spaeth argue that U.S. Supreme Court Justices are able to vote their sincere preferences because they are insulated by their status as the final arbiters on the Constitution and the fact that they enjoy life tenure.[5] Even they would be unlikely to suggest that the attitudinal model applies to judges on inferior courts where the justices are electorally accountable. These findings, however, imply that perhaps the attitudinal model is not inappropriate for the study of the decision making of these judges. While these state supreme court judges are constrained in making decisions, they do have a luxury that justices on the Supreme Court do not. State supreme court justices operate in relative obscurity. Judges may fear that their decisions will result in electoral retaliation, but in order to fear such a response, the public or other relevant government elites must be paying attention to what those judges are doing. Research on the reelection rates of state supreme court justices suggests that few judges should ever fear electoral retaliation, enjoying reelection rates comparable to, or better than, that enjoyed by members of Congress.[6] Thus even though state supreme court justices make decisions bounded by rules and norms, if they do not have reason to believe that they will be sanctioned for broaching these rules, then the power of those rules or institutions is compromised.

Overall, this research is important because it provides some insight into how interest groups participate in state supreme courts as *amici curiae*. These results are certainly not conclusive, nor are they comprehensive, but they do provide some evidence to alter the way that we look at interest group participation in the legal process. This work leaves a number of questions unanswered and allows for avenues for future research. Future studies should be expanded to include more cases over a longer time period, involving more states with differing institutional structures. Also, how might the decisions of state supreme court justices differ if the cases are confined to specific issue areas? Focusing on certain areas of the law may lead to different behavior by state supreme court justices. These issues, left for the future, should be addressed if we wish to gain a better understanding of the role played by institutions and how those rules affect the behavior of actors participating in the courts and the judges deciding those disputes.

## NOTES

1. See Lee Epstein and Jack Knight. 1998. *The Choices Justices Make.* Washington, DC: CQ Press; Lee Epstein and Jack Knight. 1999. "Mapping Out the Strategic Terrain: The Informational Role of *Amici Curiae.*" In *Supreme Court Decision-Making: New Institutional Approaches,* eds. Howard Gillman and Cornell W. Clayton.

Chicago: University of Chicago Press; James F. Spriggs II and Paul J. Wahlbeck. 1997. "*Amicus Curiae* and the Role of Information at the Supreme Court." *Political Research Quarterly* 50: 365–86.

2. Pablo T. Spiller and Richard G. VandenBergh. 1997. "A Positive Theory of State Supreme Court Decision Making." Paper presented at the 1997 annual meeting of the Midwest Political Science Association, Chicago, IL.

3. Spriggs and Wahlbeck, "*Amicus Curiae* and the Role of Information at the Supreme Court."

4. Lee Epstein and Joseph Kobylka. 1992. *The Supreme Court and Legal Change.* Chapel Hill: University of North Carolina Press; Spriggs and Wahlbeck, "*Amicus Curiae* and the Role of Information at the Supreme Court;" Lee Epstein and Jack Knight, *The Choices Justices Make.*

5. Jeffrey A. Segal and Harold J. Spaeth. 1993. *The Supreme Court and the Attitudinal Model.* Cambridge: Cambridge University Press.

6. Henry R. Glick. 1971. *Supreme Courts in State Politics.* New York: Basic Books; Melinda Gann-Hall. 2001a. "State Supreme Courts in American Democracy: Probing the Myths of Judicial Reform." *American Political Science Review* 95 (2): 315–330; Melinda Gann-Hall. 2001b. "Voluntary Retirements from State Supreme Courts: Assessing Democratic Pressures to Relinquish the Bench." *Journal of Politics* 63 (4): 1112–1140.

# APPENDIX

# The Negative Binomial Regression Model

While the Poisson is also an appropriate modeling choice for count outcomes, the data I employ do not lend themselves to this modeling technique. Of the 637 observations in the policy model, there were 164 zero outcomes. Of the 637 observations in the institutions model, there were 415 zero outcomes.

Additionally, most of the time, the conditional variance of the dependent variable is greater than its conditional mean. However, the Poisson model assumes that the conditional mean equals the conditional variance. The variance of the dependent variable in the policy model is 4.052, which is substantially larger than its mean of 2.044. The variance of the dependent variable in the institutions model is 1.736, which is larger than the mean of 0.706. In these instances, the Poisson would produce consistent but inefficient estimates. Further, the Poisson will produce downwardly biased standard errors, which would provide deceptively high z-values.[1] As a result, the most appropriate technique is the Negative Binomial Regression model which accounts for the overdispersion of the dependent variable.[2]

Some might argue that the model should be estimated using a zero inflated Poisson. To do so, one must assume that not all the zeros are qualitatively the same—some zeros may exist permanently, never having a chance to be non-zero. However, there is no reason to believe that any of the zeros are permanent. All *amici* are capable of making any number of arguments that will be of use to state supreme court justices. Therefore, there is no theoretical reason to believe that any case will *not* have a policy or institutional argument made by *amici*. While the data may be overdispersed, there is little reason to believe that the sample is truncated between zeros that are part of the count data, and those that remain zeros permanently.

## NOTES

1. J. Scott Long. 1997. *Regression Models for Categorical and Limited Dependent Variables.* Thousand Oaks, CA: Sage Publications, p. 230.

2. Long, *Regression Models;* William H. Greene. 2002. *Econometric Analysis,* 5th ed. Upper Saddle River, NJ: Prentice Hall.

# Bibliography


Abrahamson, Shirley S., and Diane S. Gutman. 1987. "The New Judicial Federalism." *Judicature* 71: 88–99.

Ainsworth, Scott, and Itai Sened. 1993. "The Role of Lobbyists: Entrepreneurs with Two Audiences." *American Journal of Political Science* 37: 834–66.

Aldrich, Howard E., Catherine R. Zimmer, Udo H. Staber, and John J. Beggs. 1994. "Minimalism, Mutualism, and Maturity: The Evolution of the American Trade Association Population in the Twentieth Century." In *Evolutionary Dynamics of Organizations,* eds. Joel A.C. Baum and Jitendra V. Singh, 223–238. New York: Oxford University Press.

Armstrong, Virginia, and Charles A. Johnson. "Certiorari Decision Making by the Warren and Burger Courts: Is Cue Theory Time Bound?" *Polity* 15 (1982): 141–50.

Arnold, Douglas R. 1990. *The Logic of Congressional Action.* New Haven: Yale University Press.

Aspin, Larry T. 1999. "Trends in Judicial Retention Elections, 1964–1998." *Judicature* 83(2): 79–81.

Aspin, Larry T., and William K. Hall. 1994. "Retention Elections and Judicial Behavior." *Judicature* 77 (6): 306–15.

Austen-Smith, David. 1993. "Information and Influence: Lobbying for Agendas and Votes." *American Journal of Political Science* 37: 799–833.

Austen-Smith, David, and John R. Wright. 1992. "Competitive Lobbying for a Legislator's Vote." *Social Choice and Welfare* 9: 229–57.

_______. 1994. "Counteractive Lobbying." *American Journal of Political Science* 38: 25–44.

_______. 1996. "Theory and Evidence for Counteractive Lobbying." *American Journal of Political Science* 40: 543–64.

Barker, Lucius. 1967. "Third Parties in Litigation: A Systematic View of the Judicial Function." *Journal of Politics* 29: 41–69.

Bass, Jack, and Walter DeVries. 1976. *The Transformation of Southern Politics: Social Change and Political Consequences Since 1945.* New York: Basic Books.

Bauer, Raymond, Ithiel de Sola Pool, and Anthony Lewis Dexter. 1963. *American Business and Public Policy.* New York: Atherton.

Baum, Lawrence. 1983. "The Electoral Fates of Incumbent Judges in the Ohio Court of Common Pleas." *Judicature* 66: 42–50.

_______. 1994. *American Courts.* Boston: Houghton Mifflin.

_______. 1994. "What Judges Want: Judges' Goals and Judicial Behavior." *Political Research Quarterly* 47: 749–68.

_______. 1997. *The Puzzle of Judicial Behavior.* Ann Arbor: University of Michigan Press.

Baumgartner, Frank R., and Beth L. Leech. 1996. "The Multiple Ambiguities of 'Counteractive Lobbying.'" *American Journal of Political Science* 40: 521–42.

Bentley, Arthur. [1908] 1967. *The Process of Government.* Cambridge: Harvard University Press.

Berry, Jeffrey M. 1977. *Lobbying for the People.* Princeton, NJ: Princeton University Press.

_______. 1997. *The Interest Group Society,* 3rd. ed. New York: Longman.

Berry, William D., Evan J. Ringquist, Richard C. Fording, and Russell L. Hanson. "Measuring Citizen and Government Ideology in the American States, 1960–93." *American Journal of Political Science* 42 (1): 327–48.

Birnbaum, Jeffrey. 1992. *The Lobbyists.* New York: Times Books.

Black, Earl, and Merle Black. 1987. *Politics and Society in the South.* Cambridge, Mass.: Harvard University Press.

Botsch, Robert E. 1992. "South Carolina: The Rise of the New South." In *Interest Group Politics in the Southern States,* eds. Ronald J. Hrebenar and Clive S. Thomas, 209–30. Tuscaloosa: University of Alabama Press.

Brace, Paul, and Melinda Gann-Hall. 1990. "Neo-Institutionalism and Dissent in State Supreme Courts." *Journal of Politics* 52: 54–70.

_______. 1995. "Studying Courts Comparatively: The View from The American States." *Political Research Quarterly* 48: 5–29.

_______. 1997. "The Interplay of Preferences, Case Facts, Context, and Rules in the Politics of Judicial Choice." *Journal of Politics* 59: 1206–31.

Brace, Paul, Laura Langer, and Melinda Gann-Hall. 2000. "Measuring the Preferences of State Supreme Court Judges." *Journal of Politics* 62 (May): 387–413.

Brace, Paul, and John A. Straayer. 1987. "Colorado: PACs, Political Candidates, and Conservatism." In *Interest Group Politics in the American West,* eds. Ronald J. Hrebenar and Clive S. Thomas. Salt Lake City: University of Utah Press.

Brennan, William J. 1977. "State Constitutions and the Protection of Individual Rights." *Harvard Law Review* 3: 489–504.

Brent, James. 1998. "State Senate Confirmations of Nominees to State Courts of Last Resort, 1980–1998." Paper presented at the Annual Meeting of the Western Political Science Association, Los Angeles, CA.

Browne, William P. 1985. "Variations in the Behavior and Style of State Lobbyists and Interest Groups." *Journal of Politics* 47 (2):450–68.

_______. 1990. "Organized Interests and their Issue Niches: A Search for Pluralism in a Policy Domain." *Journal of Politics* 52 (2): 477–509.

Browne, William P., and Delbert J. Ringquist. 1993. "Michigan: Diversity and Professionalism." In *Interest Group Politics in the Midwestern States,* eds. Ronald J. Hrebenar and Clive S. Thomas. Ames: Iowa University Press.

Caldeira, Gregory A. 1983. "On the Reputation of State Supreme Courts." *Political Behavior* 5: 83–108.

_______. 1985. "The Transmission of Legal Precedent: A Study of State Supreme Courts." *American Political Science Review* 79: 178–93.

Caldeira, Gregory A., and John R. Wright. 1988. "Organized Interests and Agenda Setting in the U.S. Supreme Court." *American Political Science Review* 82: 1109–27.

_______. 1990a. "The Discuss List: Organized Interests and Agenda-Setting." *Law and Society Review* 24: 807–36.

_______. 1990b. "*Amici Curiae* Before the Supreme Court: Who Participates, When, and How Much?" *Journal of Politics* 52: 782–806.

Caldeira, Gregory A., John R. Wright, and Christopher Zorn. 1999. "Strategic Voting and Gatekeeping in the Supreme Court." *Journal of Law, Economics and Organization* 15 (3): 549–72.

Cameron, Charles M., Albert D. Cover, and Jeffrey A. Segal. 1990. "Senate Voting on Supreme Court Nominees: A Neo-Institutional Model." *American Political Science Review* 84: 525–34.

Carbon, Susan B. 1980. "Judicial Retention Elections: Are They Serving Their Intended Purpose?" *Judicature* 64 (5): 210–33.

*Carter v. South Carolina Coastal Council* (304 S.E. 2d 327, 1986).

Cigler, Allan J., and Dwight Kiel. 1993. "Kansas: Representation in Transition." In *Interest Group Politics in the Midwestern States,* eds. Ronald J. Hrebenar and Clive S. Thomas. Ames: Iowa University Press.

Clausen, Aage R. 1973. *How Congressmen Decide: A Policy Focus.* New York: St. Martin's Press.

Cohen, Linda R., and Matthew L. Spitzer. 1994. "Solving the Chevron Puzzle." *Law and Contemporary Problems* 57 (Spring): 65–110.

Cohen, Mark A. 1992. "The Motives of Judges: Empirical Evidence from Antitrust Sentencing." *International Review of Law and Economics* 12: 13–30.

Cook, Beverly B. 1979. "Sentencing Problems and Internal Court Reform." In *The Study of Criminal Courts: Political Perspectives,* ed. Peter F. Nardulli, 227–71. Cambridge, Mass.: Ballinger Publishing Co.

Cronin, Thomas. 1989. *Direct Democracy: The Politics of Initiative, Referendum and Recall.* Cambridge: Harvard University Press.

Dahl, Robert A. 1956. *A Preface to Democratic Theory.* Chicago: University of Chicago Press.

de Tocqueville, Alexis. 1956. *Democracy in America,* ed. Richard D. Heffner. New York: Penguin.

Dolbeare, Kenneth M. 1967. *Trial Courts in Urban Politics: State Court Policy Impact and Functions in a Local Political System.* New York: John Wiley and Sons.

Dubois, Philip L. 1980. *From Bench to Ballot: Judicial Elections and the Quest for Accountability.* Austin: University of Texas Press.

Elder, Harold W. 1987. "Property Rights Structures and Criminal Courts: An Analysis of State Criminal Courts." *International Review of Law and Economics* 7 (June): 21–32.

Ennis, Bruce J. 1984. "Effective *Amicus* Briefs." *Catholic University Law Review* 33: 603–609.

Epstein, Lee. 1985. *Conservatives in Court.* Knoxville: University of Tennessee Press.

_______. 1991. "Courts and Interest Groups." In *The American Courts: A Critical Assessment,* eds. John B. Gates and Charles A. Johnson. Washington, D.C.: CQ Press.

_______. 1993. "Interest Group Litigation During the Rehnquist Court." *Journal of Law & Politics* 9 (Summer): 639–717.

_______. 1994. "Exploring the Participation of Organized Interests in State Court Litigation." *Political Research Quarterly* 47: 335–52.

Epstein, Lee, and Jack Knight. 1998. *The Choices Justices Make.* Washington: CQ Press.

_______. 1999. "Mapping Out the Strategic Terrain: The Informational Role of *Amici Curiae.*" In *Supreme Court Decision-Making: New Institutional Approaches,* eds. Howard Gillman and Cornell W. Clayton. Chicago: University of Chicago Press.

Epstein, Lee, and Joseph Kobylka. 1992. *The Supreme Court and Legal Change.* Chapel Hill: University of North Carolina Press.

Epstein, Lee, and Carol Mershon. 1996. "Measuring Political Preferences." *American Journal of Political Science* 40: 261–94.

Epstein, Lee, and C.K. Rowland. 1991. "Debunking the Myth of Interest Group Invincibility." *American Political Science Review* 85: 205–12.

Epstein, Lee, Jeffrey Segal, and Timothy Johnson. 1996. "The Claim of Issue Creation on the U.S. Supreme Court." *American Political Science Review* 34 (4): 845–52.

Epstein, Lee, Jeffrey A. Segal, Harold J. Spaeth, and Thomas G. Walker. 1998. *The Supreme Court Compendium.* Washington, DC: CQ Press.

Epstein, Lee, and Thomas G. Walker. 1995. "The Role of the Supreme Court in American Society: Playing the Reconstruction Game." In *Contemplating Courts,* ed. Lee Epstein. Washington, D.C: CQ Press.

Eskridge, William N. Jr. 1991a. "Overriding Supreme Court Statutory Interpretation Decisions." *Yale Law Journal* 101: 331–417.

_______. 1991b. "Reneging on History? Playing the Court/Congress/President Civil Rights Game." *California Law Review* 79: 613–84.

Eskridge, William N. Jr., and John Ferejohn. 1992. "The Article I, Section 7 Game." *Georgetown Law Journal* 80 (February): 523–64.

*The Federalist.* 1901. New York: M. Walter Dunne Publishers.

Fenno, Richard. 1973. *Congressmen in Committees.* Boston: Little, Brown.

Ferejohn, John, and Barry Weingast. 1992. "The Limitation of Statutes: Strategic Statutory Interpretation." *Georgetown Law Journal* 80: 565–82.

Fino, Susan P. 1987. *The Role of State Supreme Courts in the New Judicial Federalism.* New York: Greenwood Press.

Fiorina, Morris P. 1974. *Representatives, Roll Calls, and Constituencies.* Lexington, Mass.: Lexington Books.

Flango, Victor Eugene, and Craig R. Ducat. 1979. "What Difference Does Method of Judicial Selection Make?" *Justice System Journal* 5: 25–44.

Flemming, Roy B. 1982. *Punishment Before Trial: An Organizational Perspective of Felony Bail Processes.* New York: Longman.

Frank, Jerome. 1930. *Law and the Modern Mind.* New York: Coward-McCann.

Galanter, Marc, Frank S. Palen, and John M. Thomas. 1979. "The Crusading Judge: Judicial Activism in Trial Courts." *Southern California Law Review* 52: 699–741.

Gely, Rafael, and Pablo Spiller. 1990. "A Rational Choice Theory of Supreme Court Statutory Decisions with Applications to the *State Farm* & *Grove City* Cases." *Journal of Law, Economics and Organization* 6: 263–300.

_______. 1992. "The Political Economy of Supreme Court Constitutional Decisions: The Case of Roosevelt's Court Packing Plan." *International Review of Law and Economics* 12: 45–67.

Gerber, Elisabeth R. 1996. "Legislative Response to the Threat of Popular Initiatives." *American Journal of Political Science* 40 (1): 99–128.

Gibson, James L. 1978. "Judges' Role Orientations, Attitudes, and Decisions: An Interactive Model." *American Political Science Review* 72: 911–24.

_______. 1980. "Environmental Constraints on the Behavior of Judges: A Representational Model of Judicial Decision Making." *Law and Society Review* 14: 343–70.

Giles, Michael W., and Thomas G. Walker. 1975. "Judicial Policy-Making and Southern School Segregation." *Journal of Politics* 37 (November): 917–36.

Glick, Henry R. 1971. *Supreme Courts in State Politics.* New York: Basic Books.

Glick, Henry R., and Craig Emmert. 1987. "Selection Systems and Judicial Characteristics: The Recruitment of State Supreme Court Judges," *Judicature* 70: 4.

Glick, Henry R., and Kenneth N. Vines. 1973. *State Court Systems.* Englewood Cliffs, NJ: Prentice Hall.

Goldman, Sheldon. 1975. "Voting Behavior on U.S. Courts of Appeals Revisited." *American Political Science Review* 69: 491–506.

Greene, William H. 2002. *Econometric Analysis,* 5th ed. Upper Saddle River, NJ: Prentice Hall.

Griffin, Kenyon N., and Michael J. Horan. 1979. "Merit Retention Elections: What Influences the Voters?" *Judicature* 63 (2): 78–88.

Hakman, Nathan. 1969. "Lobbying the Supreme Court: An Appraisal of Political Science Folklore." *Fordham Law Review* 35: 15–50.

Hall, Melinda Gann. 1987. "Constituent Influence in State Supreme Courts: Conceptual Notes and a Case Study." *The Journal of Politics* 49: 1117–24.

_______. 1992. "Electoral Politics and Strategic Voting in State Supreme Courts." *Journal of Politics* 54: 427–46.

_______. 1995. "Justices as Representatives: Elections and Judicial Politics in the American States." *American Politics Quarterly* 23: 485–503.

_______. 2001a. "State Supreme Courts in American Democracy: Probing the Myths of Judicial Reform." *American Political Science Review* 95 (2): 315–30.

_______. 2001b. "Voluntary Retirements from State Supreme Courts: Assessing Democratic Pressures to Relinquish the Bench." *Journal of Politics* 63 (4): 1112–40.

Hall, Melinda Gann, and Paul Brace. 1989. "Order in the Courts: A Neo-Institutional Approach to Judicial Consensus." *Western Political Quarterly* 42: 391–407.

_______. 1992. "Toward an Integrated Model of Judicial Voting Behavior." *American Politics Quarterly* 20: 147–68.

_______. 1994. "The Vicissitudes of Death by Decree: Forces Influencing Capital Punishment Decision Making in State Supreme Courts." *Social Science Quarterly* 75: 136–51.

———. 1996. "Justices' Response to Case Facts: An Interactive Model." *American Politics Quarterly* 24 (2): 237–62.

———. 1999. "State Supreme Courts and Their Environments: Avenues to General Theories of Judicial Choice." In *Institutional Approaches to Supreme Court Decision Making,* eds. Cornell Clayton and Howard Gillman. Chicago: University of Chicago Press.

Hall, William, and Larry Aspin. 1987. "What Twenty Years of Judicial Retention Elections Have Taught Us." *Judicature* 70: 340–47.

Hansen, John Mark. 1991. *Gaining Access: Congress and the Farm Lobby, 1919–1981.* Chicago: University of Chicago Press.

Heclo, Hugh. 1978. "Issue Networks and the Executive Establishment." In *The New American Political System,* ed. Anthony King. Washington, DC: American Enterprise Institute.

Hedlund, Ronald D. 1993. "Wisconsin: Pressure Politics and a Lingering Progressive Tradition." In *Interest Group Politics in the Midwestern States,* eds. Ronald J. Hrebenar and Clive S. Thomas. Ames: Iowa University Press.

Heinz, John P., Edward O. Laumann, Robert L. Nelson, and Robert H. Salisbury. 1993. *The Hollow Core: Private Interests in National Policy Making.* Cambridge, MA: Harvard University Press.

Heumann, Milton. 1978. *Plea Bargaining: The Experiences of Prosecutors, Judges and Defense Attorneys.* Chicago: University of Chicago Press.

Hoekstra, Valerie. 1997. "State Supreme Courts, Policy Making and Popular Initiatives." Paper presented at the 1997 annual meeting of the American Political Science Association, Washington, DC.

Holmes, Oliver Wendell. 1881. *The Common Law.* Boston: Little Brown.

Howard, J. Woodford. 1968. "On the Fluidity of Judicial Choice." *American Political Science Review* 62: 43–56.

Hrebenar, Ronald J. 1993. "The Role of Interest Groups in Northeastern Politics." In *Interest Group Politics in the Northeastern States,* eds. Ronald J. Hrebenar and Clive S. Thomas. University Park: Pennsylvania State University Press.

Jacobson, Gary C. 1987. "The Marginals Never Vanished: Incumbency and Competition in Elections to the U.S. House of Representatives, 1952–1982." *American Journal of Political Science* 31: 126–41.

Johnson, Timothy. 1998. *Oral Advocacy and the Supreme Court.* Unpublished doctoral dissertation, Washington University, St. Louis, MO.

"Judicial Selection in the States: A Critical Study with Proposals for Reform." 1976. *Hofstra Law Review* 4: 267–320.

Key, V.O. Jr. [1949] 1993. *Southern Politics in State and Nation.* Knoxville: University of Tennessee Press.

Kingdon, John W. 1981. *Congressmen's Voting Decisions.* 2d. ed. New York: Harper & Row.

Knight, Jack. 1992. *Institutions and Social Conflict.* New York: Cambridge University Press.

Knight, Jack, and Lee Epstein. 1996. "On the Struggle for Judicial Supremacy." *Law and Society Review* 30: 87–120.

Krislov, Samuel. 1963. "The *Amicus Curiae* Brief: From Friendship to Advocacy." *Yale Law Journal* 7: 694–721.

Kuklinski, James, and John Stanga. 1979. "Political Participation and Governmental Responsiveness: The Behavior of California Superior Courts." *American Political Science Review* 73: 1090–99.

Langbein, Laura. 1986. "Money and Access: Some Empirical Evidence." *Journal of Politics* 48: 1052–62.

Langer, Laura. 2002. *Judicial Review in State Supreme Courts: A Comparative Study.* Albany: State University of New York Press.

Latzer, Barry. 1991. "The Hidden Conservatism of the State Court Revolution." *Judicature* 74: 190–97.

Llewellyn, Karl. 1960. *The Common Law Tradition: Deciding Appeals.* Boston: Little, Brown.

Long, J. Scott. 1997. *Regression Models for Categorical and Limited Dependent Variables.* Thousand Oaks, CA: Sage Publications.

Lutz, Donald. 1994. "Toward a Theory of Constitutional Amendment." *American Political Science Review* 88: 355–70.

Magleby, David B. 1984. *Direct Legislation: Voting on Ballot Propositions in the United States.* Baltimore: Johns Hopkins University Press.

Maltzman, Forrest, and Paul Wahlbeck. 1996. "Strategic Policy Considerations and Voting Fluidity on the Burger Court." *American Political Science Review* 90 (September): 581–92.

Mann, Thomas E. 1978. *Unsafe at Any Margin: Interpreting Congressional Elections.* Washington, DC: American Enterprise Institute for Public Policy Research.

Marks, Brian A. 1989. *A Model of Judicial Influence on Congressional Policymaking: Grove City College v. Bell.* Unpublished doctoral dissertation, Washington University, St. Louis, MO.

Martin, Andrew. 1998. *Strategy, and The Separation of Powers.* Unpublished doctoral dissertation, Washington University, St. Louis, MO.

Martin, David L. 1978. "PAC Money in State Legislative Elections: An Alabama Report." *Comparative State Politics Newsletter* 8(4): 18–21.

_______. 1992. "Alabama: Personalities and Factionalism." In *Interest Group Politics in the Southern States,* eds. Ronald J. Hrebenar and Clive S. Thomas. 249–67. Tuscaloosa: University of Alabama Press.

Matsusaka, John G. 1995. "Fiscal Effects of the Voter Initiative: Evidence from the Last 30 Years." *Journal of Political Economy* 103: 587–623.

Mayhew, David R. 1974. *Congress: The Electoral Connection.* New Haven, Conn.: Yale University Press.

_______. 1986. *Placing Parties in American Politics.* Princeton: Princeton University Press.

Maxwell, Robert S. 1956. *La Follette and the Rise of the Progressives in Wisconsin.* Madison: State Historical Society of Wisconsin.

McCubbins, Matthew D., Roger G. Noll, and Barry R. Weingast. 1992. "Positive Canons: The Role of Legislative Bargains in Statutory Interpretation." *Georgetown Law Journal,* Vol. 809 (February): 705–742.

McGuire, Kevin T., and Gregory A. Caldeira. 1993. "Lawyers, Organized Interests, and the Law of Obscenity: Agenda Setting in the Supreme Court." *American Political Science Review* 87: 717–26.

McGuire, Kevin, and Barbara Palmer. 1995. "Issue Fluidity on the U.S. Supreme Court." *American Political Science Review* 89(3): 691–702.

Milbrath, Lester. 1960. "Lobbying as a Communication Process." *Public Opinion Quarterly* 24: 32–53.

Moe, Terry. 1980. *The Organization of Interests.* Chicago: University of Chicago Press.

Morehouse, Sarah McCally. 1981. *State Politics, Parties and Policy.* New York: Holt, Rinehart and Winston.

Murphy, Walter. 1964. *Elements of Judicial Strategy.* Chicago: University of Chicago Press.

Neubauer, David W. 1974. *Criminal Justice in Middle America.* Morristown, NJ: General Learning Press.

Neustadt, Richard E. 1990. *Presidential Power and the Modern Presidents: The Politics of Leadership from Roosevelt to Reagan.* New York: Free Press.

O'Connor, Karen. 1980. *Women's Organizations' Use of the Courts.* Lexington, Mass.: Lexington Books.

O'Connor, Karen, and Lee Epstein. 1981–82. "*Amicus Curiae* Participation in U.S. Supreme Court Litigation: An Analysis of Hakman's 'Folklore.'" *Law and Society Review* 16: 312–20.

_______. 1983. "The Rise of Conservative Interest Group Litigation." *Journal of Politics* 45: 479–89.

_______. 1989. *Public Interest Law Groups.* New York: Greenwood Press.

O'Connor, Karen, and Bryant Scott McFall. 1992. "Conservative Interest Group Litigation in the Reagan Era and Beyond." In *The Politics of Interests: Interest Groups Transformed,* ed. Mark P. Petracca. Boulder, CO: Westview Press.

Olson, Mancur. 1965. *The Logic of Collective Action.* Cambridge, MA: Harvard University Press.

_______. 1982. *The Rise and Decline of Nations.* New Haven, CT: Yale University Press.

Peirce, Neal R. 1972. *The Deep South States of America.* New York: W.W. Norton.

_______. 1972. *The Mountain States of America.* New York: W.W. Norton.

_______. 1973. *The Great Plains States of America.* New York: W.W. Norton.

Peirce, Neal R., and Jerry Hagstrom. 1983. *The Book of America: Inside 50 States Today.* New York: W.W. Norton.

Perry, H.W. Jr. 1991. *Deciding to Decide: Agenda Setting in the United States Supreme Court.* Cambridge, MA: Harvard University Press.

Petracca, Mark. 1992. "The Rediscovery of Interest Group Politics." In *The Politics of Interests: Interest Groups Transformed,* ed. Mark P. Petracca. Boulder, CO: Westview Press.

Polsby, Nelson W. 1964. *Congress and the Presidency.* Englewood Cliffs, NJ: Prentice-Hall.

Price, Charles M. 1980. "The Initiative: A Comparative State Analysis and Reassessment of a Western Phenomenon." *Western Political Quarterly* 28: 243–62.

Pritchett, C. Herman. 1948. *The Roosevelt Court.* New York: MacMillan.

Rohde, David W., and Harold J. Spaeth. 1976. *Supreme Court Decision Making.* San Francisco: W.H. Freedman.

Rosenberg, Gerald. 1991. *The Hollow Hope: Can Courts Bring About Social Change?* Chicago: University of Chicago Press.

Rosenthol, Alan, and Maureen Moakley. 1984. *The Political Life of the American States.* New York: Praeger.

Salisbury, Robert H. 1969. "An Exchange Theory of Interest Groups." *Midwest Journal of Political Science* 3:1–32.

_______. 1975. "Interest Groups." In *Handbook of Political Science, Vol. 4,* eds. I. Greenstein and Nelson W. Polsby. Reading, Mass.: Addison-Wesley.

_______. 1984. "Interest Representation: The Dominance of Institutions." *American Political Science Review* 78: 64–76.

_______. 1990. "The Paradox of Interest Groups in Washington, DC: More Groups and Less Clout." In *The New American Political System,* 2d version, ed. Anthony S. King. Washington, DC: American Enterprise Institute.

Salmore, Barbara G., and Stephen A. Salmore. 1993. "New Jersey: From Political Hacks to Political Action Committees." In *Interest Group Politics in the Northeastern States,* eds. Ronald J. Hrebenar and Clive S. Thomas. University Park: Pennsylvania State University Press.

Schlozman, Kay Lehmann, and John Tierney. 1986. *Organized Interests and American Democracy.* New York: Harper & Row.

Schmidhauser, John R. 1964. "The Background Characteristics of United States Supreme Court Justices." In *Judicial Behavior: A Reader in Theory and Research,* ed. Glendon Schubert. Chicago: Rand McNally.

Schubert, Glendon. 1958. "The Study of Judicial Decision-Making as an Aspect of Political Behavior." *American Political Science Review* 52:1007–25.

_______. 1965. *The Judicial Mind: The Attitudes and Ideologies of Supreme Court Justices, 1946–1963.* Evanston: Northwestern University Press.

Segal, Jeffrey A. 1997. "Separation-of-Powers Games in the Positive Theory of Congress and the Courts." *American Political Science Review* 91: 28–44.

Segal, Jeffrey A., and Albert Cover. 1989. "Ideological Values and the Votes of U.S. Supreme Court Justices." *American Political Science Review* 83: 557–65.

Segal, Jeffrey A., Donald R. Songer, and Charles M. Cameron. 1994. "The Hierarchy of Justice: Testing a Principal-Agent Model of Supreme Court-Circuit Court Interactions." *American Journal of Political Science* 38: 673–96.

_______. 1995. "Decision Making on the U.S. Courts of Appeals." In *Contemplating Courts,* ed. Lee Epstein. Washington, D.C.: CQ Press.

Segal, Jeffrey A., and Harold J. Spaeth. 1993. *The Supreme Court and the Attitudinal Model.* Cambridge: Cambridge University Press.

Sheldon, Charles, and Linda Maule. 1997. *Choosing Justice: The Recruitment of State and Federal Judges.* Pullman: Washington State University Press.

Shepsle, Kenneth A., and Mark Bonchek. 1997. *Analyzing Politics.* New York: Norton.

Songer, Donald R. 1979. "Concern for Policy Outputs as a Cue for Supreme Court Decisions on Certiorari." *Journal of Politics* 41:1185–94.

_______. 1990. "An Overview of Judicial Policymaking in the United States Courts of Appeals." In *The American Courts: A Critical Assessment,* eds. John B. Gates and Charles A. Johnson. Washington, DC: Congressional Quarterly.

Songer, Donald R., and Reginald S. Sheehan. 1993. "Interest group success in the courts: *Amicus* participation in the Supreme Court." *Political Research Quarterly* 46 (2): 339–55.

Songer, Donald R., and Susan J. Tabrizi. 1999. "The Religious Right in Court: The Decision Making of Christian Evangelicals in State Supreme Courts." *Journal of Politics* 61 (2): 507–26.

Sorauf, Frank J. 1976. *The Wall of Separation: Constitutional Politics of Church and State.* Princeton, NJ: Princeton University Press.

Spiller, Pablo T., and Rafael Gely. 1992. "Congressional Control or Judicial Independence: The Determinants of U.S. Supreme Court Labor Relations Decisions, 1949–1988." *RAND Journal of Economics* 23:463–92.

Spiller, Pablo T., and Richard G. VandenBergh. 1997. "A Positive Theory of State Supreme Court Decision Making." Paper presented at the 1997 annual meeting of the Midwest Political Science Association, Chicago, IL.

Spriggs, James F. II, Forrest Maltzman, and Paul J. Wahlbeck. 1999. "Bargaining on the U.S. Supreme Court: Justices: Responses to Majority Opinion Drafts." *Journal of Politics* 61 (May): 485–506.

Spriggs, James F. II, and Paul J. Wahlbeck. 1997. "*Amicus Curiae* and the Role of Information at the Supreme Court." *Political Research Quarterly* 50: 365–86.

*State v. Gerhardstein* (416 N.W. 2d 883, 1987).

Sullivan, Richard. 1986. "Environmental Policy." In *The Political State of New Jersey* ed. Gerald Pomper. New Brunswick, NJ: Rutgers University Press.

Tarr, G. Alan, and Mary Cornelia Aldis Porter. 1982. "Gender Equality and Judicial Federalism: The Role of State Appellate Courts." *Hastings Constitutional Law Quarterly* 9: 919.

_______. 1988. *State Supreme Courts in State and Nation.* New Haven: Yale University Press.

Thomas, Clive S. 1992. "Understanding Interest Group Activity." In *Interest Group Politics in the Southern States,* eds. Ronald J. Hrebenar and Clive S. Thomas. University Park: Pennsylvania State University Press.

Thomas, James D., and William H. Stewart. 1988. *Alabama Government and Politics.* Lincoln: University of Nebraska Press.

Truman, David B. 1951. *The Governmental Process: Political Interests and Public Opinion.* New York: Knopf.

Vose, Clement E. 1959. *Caucasians Only.* Berkeley: University of California Press.

_______. 1972. *Constitutional Change.* Lexington, Mass.: Lexington Books.

Wahlbeck, Paul J. 1997. "The Life of the Law: Judicial Politics and Legal Change." *Journal of Politics* 59 (August): 778–802.

Wahlbeck, Paul J., James F. Spriggs II, and Forrest Maltzman. 1998. "Marshalling the Court: Bargaining and Accommodation on the United States Supreme Court." *American Journal of Political Science* 42 (January): 294–315.

Walker, Jack L. 1983. "The Origins and Maintenance of Interest Groups in America." *American Political Science Review* 77: 390–406.

_______. 1991. *Mobilizing Interest Groups in America: Patrons, Professionals, and Social Movements.* Ann Arbor: University of Michigan Press.

Wasby, Stephen L. 1984. "How Planned is 'Planned Litigation'?" *1984 American Bar Foundation Research Journal* 83–138.

Watson, Richard A., and Ronald G. Downing. 1969. *The Politics of Bench and Bar: Judicial Selection under the Missouri Nonpartisan Court Plan.* New York: Wiley.

Weissman, Dan. "Fourth Branch of Government: Lobbyists Play Pivotal Role in Legislative Action." *Newark Star Ledger,* March 22, 1987.

Wilson, James Q. 1973. *Political Organizations.* New York: Basic Books.

Wolbrecht, Christina. 1994. "Separation of Powers, Constitutional Interpretation, and the Free Exercise of Religion: A Formal Model." Washington University Political Science Working Paper.

Wold, John T., and John H. Culver. 1987. "The Defeat of the California Justices: The Campaign, the Electorate, and the Issue of Judicial Accountability." *Judicature* 70: 348–55.

Wright, John R. 1996. *Interest Groups and Congress: Lobbying, Contributions, and Influence.* Boston: Allyn and Bacon.

Zeigler, L. Harmon. 1983. "Interest Groups in the States." In *Politics in the American States.* 4th ed., eds. Virginia Gray, Herbert Jacob, and Kenneth Vines. Boston: Little, Brown.

Zeigler, L. Harmon, and Michael Baer. 1969. *Lobbying: Interaction and Influence in American State Legislatures.* Belmont, CA: Wadsworth.

Zeller, Belle. 1954. *American State Legislatures.* 2d ed. New York: Thomas Crowell.

# Index

**About the Author**

SCOTT A. COMPARATO is Assistant Professor of Political Science at Southern Illinois University–Carbondale. His primary research interests center on judicial decision-making and state supreme courts.